Decision-Making
and Law

Decision-Making
and Law

Normative Rationality or Evolutive Rationality?

Edited by
Silvia Dell'Orco

sussex
ACADEMIC
PRESS
Brighton • Portland • Toronto

2 4 6 8 10 9 7 5 3 1

First published in 2018 in Great Britain by
SUSSEX ACADEMIC PRESS
PO Box 139
Eastbourne BN24 9BP

Distributed in North America by
SUSSEX ACADEMIC PRESS
ISBS Publisher Services
920 NE 58th Ave #300, Portland, OR 97213, USA

British Library Cataloguing in Publication Data
A CIP catalogue record for this book is available from the British Library.

Library of Congress Cataloging-in-Publication Data
Names: Dell'Orco, Silvia, editor.
Title: Decision-making and law : normative rationality or evolutive
    rationality? / [edited by] Silvia Dell'Orco.
Description: Brighton ; Portland : Sussex Academic Press, [2018] | Includes
    bibliographical references.
Identifiers: LCCN 2017053179 | ISBN 9781845199128 (pbk : alk. paper)
Subjects: LCSH: Decision-making. | Canon law.
Classification: LCC BF448 .D4188 2018 | DDC 153.8/3—dc23
LC record available at https://lccn.loc.gov/2017053179

Typeset and designed by Sussex Academic Press, Brighton & Eastbourne.

Contents

Introduction

SILVIA DELL'ORCO

In general, a decision (from Latin *de-cisio-onis*: "separating", "cutting") can be defined as a response to a situation characterized by at least three components: 1) The decision maker must have the opportunity to evaluate more than one course of action or alternative; 2) the decision maker must have expectations relative to the possibility that the events associated with each course of action come true, producing determinate results; 3) finally, there must be consequences associated with possible outcomes, which be assessed based on the personal values and goals of the decision maker.

Every day we take more or less important decisions. Some of them are accomplished automatically and instantly, while others involve more articulate evaluations and reasoning as well as specific knowledge. Often, during the decision-making process, we are influenced by misleading ideas about the surrounding reality and making mistakes, especially when confronted with uncertain and risky situations. In fact, unlike problem solving, decision is the outcome of a process that highlight, the will, the emotions, the responsibility, the awareness, the action.

However, how does our mind act in choosing between different alternatives? For some time, philosophers, psychologists, economists, and mathematicians face the question of how people decide or how they should do it. The statisticians, with mathematical formulas that allow accurate estimates of probabilities. The economists with predictive models of individual and collective choices that affect market performance. The psychologists with the study of the ways in which people make choices that take into account the constraints of the cognitive system and so on. In fact, not all theories and experimental research programs have passed the judgment of time. Nevertheless, they have contributed to the definition of a complex argumentative architecture that, simultaneously to a great deal of empirical, psychological, cognitive and neuroscientific evidence, is today the basis of what many define a true science of decision-making.

It is a transdisciplinary research area, within which at least two major theoretical approaches are recognized. On the one hand, there is the economic paradigm, characterized by so-called normative theories. The latter point to the ideal decision criterions who, completely rational informed individuals provided with perfect abilities of argument, that should followed to make the best decision or choose the best means to achieve a certain end. On the other hand, there is the descriptive approach of psychology that moving from empirical findings that not always individuals behave in an optimal way are intended to describe decision-making mechanisms in *real world* situations, characterized by time constraints, lack or excess of information as well as limited cognitive resources. The latter are diametrically opposed to normative theories: what matters is not the "predictive goodness" of a theory, but rather its "adherence to reality", its disposition to openness, to change. Reducing decision-making to mere problem solving exercise is, in fact, a simplification that bestows the character of the model's generality, but has a lack of realistic not negligible. This that will lead the birth of Behavioral Economics, will be the wide debate on the uncertainty that accompanies the economic decisions, on the tools which the human rationality dispose to affront and on an extensive knowledge of logic that includes, as well as the deductive inferences, also not deductive, not propositional, unconscious, heuristic..

It is difficult, in fact, to escape the impression that a normative interpretation of human action, though mathematically consistent, leaves unresolved and unexplored countless issues related to the 'real behavior of the subject'. The voluntariness of the assumption and evaluation of the risk, personality, decision-making styles, personality traits, fear for possible consequences on the future, courage of the decision-maker and more.

This will be the thread, in the mid-twentieth century, which will guide the attack of psychologists, but also of the same economists, of the theoretic ruler of the decision-maker, underlining the serious limitations of its applications and revealing some systematic violations of regulatory axioms. In everyday life, the decision-maker moves away from the *homo oeconomicus* model, showing inconsistency in preferences and limits in cognitive abilities. He, for example, can be influenced by how you are mentally represented a decision problem and its choices can be manipulated depending on how the information is presented.

The study of these factors has stimulated, especially since the end of the last century, the birth of new research programs. An example is *Naturalistic Decision Making*, a paradigm of research that studies how people decide and perform complex cognitive functions in real world contexts, in all those situations characterized by time pressure, incomplete knowledge of alternatives, emotional tension, uncertainty, bad goals, high stakes, and different degrees of decision maker experience. To study the way you make a decision does not just mean to investigate how much it meets the *Anticipated Utility*, but to evaluate the natural procedures followed by the decision makers before taking a certain course of action. These procedures consist of three basic principles:

1. Every decision, be taken after a holistic assessment of potential alternatives, and not comparing specific features.
2. The decider chooses not based on the search and detailed elaboration of all available alternatives, but by recognizing the situation by comparing alternatives and potential action.
3. The decision makers do not aim at achieving an optimal solution, but adopt a criterion of choice *satisficing*.

The obvious asymmetries between the patterns of rational choice and the concrete behavior of the people emerge also in the canonical law, with the manifestation in the matrimonial institute of consensus that may be subject, for example, to coercive influences, aimed at spoiling the liberty expression of the will of the intending spouse. In this book, therefore, we will examine not only some possible defects in matrimonial consent, but also the informal choice criteria   determined by the interference of cognitive and contextual elements in the assessment of the problem and available information in order to try to deal situations with a wide degree of uncertainty.

1

Optimizers *versus* Satisficers: Decision-making Styles, Heuristics and Ecological Rationality

NELSON MAURO MALDONATO, SILVIA DELL'ORCO,
RAFFAELE SPERANDEO, NICOLE NASCIVERA

Over the last half century, an increasing number of experimental research on decision-making has investigated systemic deviations from the axioms of the *expected utility*, so that people would always be in a position to consider in depth all the available decision-making options in terms of probability (*expectations*) that of values (*utilities*) (Loewenstein 2001). Such researches has highlighted the unacceptability of an abstract rationality that does not consider limits neither of the external environment (*task environment*) nor the cognitive ones of the human being. Around the middle of the twentieth century, while many economists supported the argument that individuals decide only after having carried out the complex calculations required by the normative model. Herbert Simon (1983) opens up a gap in psychological and economic reflection, arguing that a decision does not represent the result of a simple algorithmic data processing, but an adaptive process, which allows you to achieve a dynamic balance between an effective fast and economical action and a configuration that reality should have because of the resolution of one problem. As you know, at base of the Simon's *bounded rationality* there is the idea that the human decisions not governed by logical-formal procedures, but by heuristics. Are cognitive devices that, on the one hand, can generate distortions (*biases*), on the other, are extremely effective tools used by the human mind to reduce cognitive load and respond quickly to problems posed by the environment (Hamilton, Gifford 1976). In other words, these are reasoning strategies not deliberated, which allow the individual to make sustainable choices for computing and processing congruous information with the complexity of the situation. Simon's ideas will pave the way for a wide range of experimental researches on the "deviations" of individual behaviors from predictions of neoclassical economic theory: researches that will have strongly relaunched by Kahneman and Tversky, who will show strictly the non-randomness and systematic nature of such deviations. Unlike the neoclassical theory that considered information as a scarce and negotiable good (like any generic good or production factor) several authors (Marschak, Radner 1972) make it clear that it is not only scarce but above all that, under superabundance , may not be perceived and elaborated by decision makers. Overabundance, complexity, heterogeneity, and limited subjective interpretative capacities of information revoke the neoclassical analysis of information (Stigler 1961), which states that the latter is measurable in terms of cost-benefit analysis. Since inconsistencies in expectations and cognitive incompleteness – generated by the scarcity or excess of information to be processed – characterize the most varied contexts of individual choice, the decision maker must adapt to flexible conditions by using learning operations that reduce complexity of the calculations required for the decision.

In the descriptive approach to decision-making, individual choices are determined not only by some complete and consistent objectives and by the properties of the outside world, but also by the knowledge that decision makers have in the world, their ability to evoke such knowledge at the right time, of elaborate the consequences of their actions, of anticipate the course of the events, of face up the uncertainties (including those arising from the possible reactions or responses of other actors involved) and finally choosing between their different needs in competition (Simon 1997). In this sense, because of the high adaptive value of the reasoning, that determines it, *bounded rationality*, that cannot be considered irrational, nor can it be invoked only to explain human error.

As Selten observed (1998), it is possible to construct theories of limited rationality in which behavior, albeit not optimizing, is far from irrational. If in a rational order absolute, the alternatives are given in a rational order limited these must be made-up from time to time by the agent, in a process that generates many possible actions (Simon 1997). As far as the enterprise, the species biological or even more, adaptation to their respective environments always depends, according to Simon, by a heuristic research and local optimization forms or *satisficing* (Simon 1983). The search of alternative ends with what, depending on the circumstances, best meets our goals and needs. In this sense, an evolutionary theory of rationality must contemplate a theory of research that does not adhere to the rule of "normative arrest" (March 1994) – according to which the search for alternatives ends only after achieving an ideal optimizing result – but focuses on the personal aspiration levels.

Heuristics and Biases Approach

Starting with Simon's research, *Behavioral Economics* attempts to integrate classical theory of rational choice with new hypotheses from psychology – particularly that experimental – shifting attention from the substantive rationality to procedural rationality. Search and satisficing (Simon 1979) are the crux terms of the decision-making process with limited rationality: agents review by serial the decision-making alternatives at disposal and stop when such a research reaches a determinate threshold (also only implicit) of satisfaction. Dealing with a business decision, an individual behaves like the chess player who must choose the move. Both the economist and the chess player reasoning according to procedures. However, the winning strategy be constructed by degrees, not preventively, according to a tree diagram, reformulated from time to time based on the countermoves of the opponent. In addition, in economics, as in chess games, success is often due the fact that humans are simply endow with good intuitions and effective judgment (Simon 1983; Kasparov 2008).

In the seventies, Kahneman and Tversky, through Heuristics and Biases Approach research program, gave a scientific foundation to the concept of heuristics, which has become the hub of a realistic model of rational agent. Through the provision of appropriately thought-out decision-making problems, to samples of individuals, the objective of scholars was to test if they were considering and deciding according to the formal criterions of reasoning. In the view of Kahneman, Slovic and Tversky (1982), heuristic judgment is often the only way to make a decision of uncertainty. Unlike formal reasoning, the heuristic evaluation of probability is based on immediate solutions that consider only a few of the factors involved: the peculiar characteristics of the evaluation object, the way the problem is formulated, the clarity with which it is described the situation and so on. Factors, these, which influence separately or in a combined manner on the final decision.

These researches if, on the one hand, provided important clues on the nature of human cognitive processes (contributing to weakening the model of *homo oeconomicus*), on the other hand they devalued the term 'heuristic' because of its strong connections to the concept of *bias*. In fact, the latter is generally defined as the difference between human judgment and a rational norm, often regarded as a law of logical probability; almost as if one *bias* internal to human reasoning was avoided, it would be possible to make optimal decisions. Through the so-called dual process theory, Kahneman and Tversky have shown how people, in making a judgment or decision, recourse to two different cognitive systems: intuitive processes (system 1: primitive, fast and associative) and analytic processes (system 2: slow, serial and deductive) (Kahneman, Frederick 2002; Stanovich 1999). System 1 produces a quick response that be subsequently approved, correct or replaced by system 2 (though rather infrequent). In the process of message comprehension, attributes highly accessible to system 1 (similarity, availability, affection) become heuristic attributes for the final judgment. In other words, intuitive judgment is activated if you use a very accessible attribute (elaborated by perception or by system 1), and if system 2 control fails.

Towards an Ecological Rationality

The recognition the limits of human rationality laid the foundations for the emergence of a very new approach to the study of decisions (Maldonato 2010). An example is the birth, at the end of last century, of *Naturalistic Decision Making* (NDM), research paradigm that he studies the way in which the persons decide and carry complex cognitive functions out in the contexts real world, that is, in all that situations characterised by temporal pressures, incomplete knowledge of the alternatives, emotional tension, uncertainty, objectives badly definite, high stakes and different degrees of experience of the of decision-maker. To study the way you make a choice does not just mean to investigate how much it meets the *Expected Utility*, but to evaluate the natural procedures followed by the decision makers before taking a particular action. These procedures have three basic principles:

1. Every decision is made after a holistic evaluation of potential alternatives, and not by comparing the specific characteristics (Lipshitz *et al.* 2001);
2. The decision maker does not act on the basis of the search and detailed elaboration of the alternatives, but through the the recognition of the situation *(recognition-based)* approach which is made by comparing alternatives and potential courses of action *(pattern-matching)*;
3. Decision makers do not aim at achieving an optimal solution, but adopt a choice criterion (satisficing) (Klein, Calderwood 1991).

The ability of individuals to make adaptive choices – by modifying their cognitive strategies based on context and structural changes in decision-making – suggests a *sufficiently* optimistic picture for *decision makers* in terms of behavioral rationality (Payne, Bettman, Johnson 1993). This prompted Gigerenzer to review the classic heuristic concept proposed by Kahneman and Tversky. If, for the latter, heuristics are cognitive strategies that cause biases and affect the taking of correct decisions over regulatory standards, the heuristics of the German psychologist are fast and frugal, perfectly adaptive strategies that work within environmental constraints (limited time, insufficient information, etc.) and cognitive-computational of decision maker (Tietz 1992).

These strategies are based on three basic rules:

1. *Search rule*: the heuristics directs the search for the information and the decision-making alternatives in a limited time and without making any calculations;
2. *Stopping rule*: Specifies how and when the search procedure have to be interrupt. In line with the In line with the Simon's theory of the *bounded rationality*, given the cognitive and environmental limits of *real world* problems, arrest happens on the base on satisfactory processes (Richardson 1998) and non-optimizing;
3. *Heuristic principles*: Quick and adaptive decision procedures that, however, can be very precise with respect to classical algorithmic computation.

It is evident that the correspondence between the mind of the decision maker and the environment is the turning point of an ecological redefinition of rationality (Todd, Gigerenzer 2000). In other words, if in the inferential approach are considered, by compensatory way, all the available attributes, in the ecological approach there are no mathematical or average calculations since the characteristics of each option are considered in non-compensatory way. This type of *fast and frugal* heuristic research is based on a stop rule defined as *one reason*, according to which the choice of option based on a single clue and information that meets an optimal criterion for the decision-maker. In that case, it is about *ignorance-based decision making*, which is generally the first stage of all decisions of type *one-reason*. The importance of this heuristic family lies precisely in the type of ecological rationality underlying their process. In fact, in line with the Simon's system, in particular with regard to the adaptive aspect with which decision-makers choose their courses of action, Gigerenzer (2001) proposes the metaphor of the *Adaptive Toolbox*. This is a kind of "toolbox" consisting by a repertory of heuristics, acquired evolutionarily, which possess the following characteristics:

(1) they are specialized in certain tasks;
(2) f rom the computational point of view they are simple, frugal and fast;
(3) they do not have the problem of formal consistency, but rather that of adaptive effectiveness;
(4) solve immediate problems linked to the challenges posed by the environment (getting food, avoiding predators, finding a partner and a safe haven, but also, at a higher level, exchanging goods, making profits, and so on;
(5) while performing this task, heuristic can replaced.

To describe the nature of the "toolbox", Gigerenzer (2001) uses the image of a mechanic and a seller of used parts of an isolated region that does not have the tools and has not all the spare parts but faces problem and tries to find a solution with the tools it has. These acquired capabilities in evolutionary way, according to Gigerenzer, constitute the metal of which the tools are made; and a visceral feel is such as a drill, a rather simple tool whose strength lies in the quality of the material. These tools work well in natural situations, where the presence of time constraints, knowledge and computational capabilities make winning the adoption of rapid and effective strategies. It is clear that, freed by with the traditional negative connotation, heuristic strategies more than deviations from a rational "norm", they respond to an ecological and adaptive rationality that allows the individual to effectively deal with situations of uncertainty, information incompleteness, and risk, typical of the reality we live in.

Decision-making Styles

Another research model developed under the NDM defined *recognition-primed*. Starting from expert decisions (doctors, firefighters, military commanders, pilots, and more) Klein and colleagues (1993) have shown that in critical situations – characterized by drastic temporal constraints and serious consequences – they do not follow normative models. Think, for example, of what could happen if, in an emergency, the commander of firefighters patrol did not decide effectively and in a matter of seconds on what to do. Certainly, it would jeopardize the lives of many people. In such situations is not always the purpose of being clear (to secure people or quickly extinguish the fire?). The information is not always certain (you may not have a clear idea of the plan of the building where it broke out the fire or the material contained therein) and intervention procedures are not always encoded (sometimes it is necessary to act by instinct to find a way to free a wounded car after an accident).

Recognition based decision models (Klein 1998) move from counterintuitive observation, which experts decide without analytically assessing the pros and cons of each option: in fact, beginners decide on an analytical-comparative basis. In fact, when an expert in a given field has to make a decision, he quickly returns to situations and experiences already known. Quickly identify the goals be pursued, the most important clues to observe and monitor, the possible evolution of the situation and the action plans to follow. In other words, the evaluation of the effectiveness of the selected course of action (or, better, automatically recalled) is not done by comparison with other actions, but by finding a plausible and, therefore, satisfactory solution. However, individual differences in decision-making affect not only the degree of expertise but also other variables such as cognitive and motivational orientations, age, gender, socio-economic status, and more. For example, some authors have hypothesized the existence of real decision-making styles that define a general propensity of the subject to adopt a cognitive strategy more frequently than in others (Riding, Glass, Douglas 1993). This propensity, therefore, influences in a relatively stable manner how each individual makes choices (Stanovich, West 1998, Schwartz et al. 2002, Scott, Bruce 1995). Over the years, many cognitive and decision-making styles been identified and described, which often relate to a kind of bipolarity. Such as the tendency to be independent / context dependent (Witkin 1962) or the preference for a serial processing rather than holistic (Pask 1972). Other dimensions emphasize preference for certain structural properties used in the elaborated case of the information, or even between impulsive and reflective style (Kagan et al. 1964), between deliberative and intuitive style (Epstein 1996), among adapters and innovators (Kirton 1976) between assimilators and explorers (Kaufmann 1979) and so on.

Other types of decision-making styles more articulated, however, have multiple dimensions. Scott and Bruce (1995) identify five different decision styles:

- rational style: it is characterized by a comprehensive search of information, considering possible alternatives and evaluating their consequences;
- intuitive style: it is based on attention to global aspects rather than systematic processing of information and, moreover, the tendency to decide based on intuitions and sensations;
- dependent style: It is typical of people who prefer to receive suggestions before making any choice;
- elusive style: It is typical of people who tend to postpone or escape any decision;

- spontaneous style: be characterized by the propensity to decide as quickly as possible.

To define and measure the individual decision-making profile, Scott and Bruce have finalized *General Decision Making Style* (1995). Another way to distinguish between different decision-making styles is that proposed by Schwartz and his research group (2002), which more than identify a specific decision-making style, have deepened the dynamics that drive an individual to seek the best possible result (the "maximizer") or, rather, to settle for a sufficiently good alternative (the "satisfiers"). To this end, they have developed the *Maximization Scale* (Schwartz et al. 2002). A tool to distinguish those who tend to base their decisions on confrontation with others, showing themselves unhappy with the choice made and those who, by having a sufficiently good option, and therefore not necessarily the best, show a good level of satisfaction compared to own decision. There it is be said that over one century ago James had already outlined an outline of the decision-making types.

The first may be called the reasonable type. It is that of those cases in which the arguments for and against a given course seem gradually and almost insensibly to settle themselves in the mind and to end by leaving a clear balance in favour of one alternative, which alternative we then adopt without effort or constraint [...]. A "reasonable" character is one who has a store of stable and worthy ends, and who does not decide about an action till he has calmly ascertained whether it be ministerial or detrimental to any one of these [...]. In the second type of case our feeling is to a certain extent that of letting ourselves drift with a certain indifferent acquiescence in a direction accidentally determined from without, with the conviction that, after all, we might as well stand by this course as by the other, and that things are in any event sure to turn out sufficiently right. In the third type, the determination seems equally accidental, but it comes from within, and not from without [...]. There is a fourth form of decision, which often ends deliberation as suddenly as the third form does. It comes when, in consequence of some outer experience or some inexplicable inward change, we suddenly pass from the easy and careless to the sober and strenuous mood, or possibly the other way [...]. All those "changes of heart", "awakenings of conscience", etc., which make new men of so many of us, may be classed under this head [...]. In the fifth and final type of decision, the feeling that the evidence is all in, and that reason has balanced the books, may be either present or absent. But in either case we feel, in deciding, as if we ourselves by our own wilful act inclined the beam: in the former case by adding our living effort to the weight of the logical reason which, taken alone, seems powerless to make the act discharge; in the latter by a kind of creative contribution of something instead of a reason which does a reason's work. [James 1950, pp. 796–798]

Recently, the focus of research in decision-making styles has shifted from the description and description of such styles to their study as predictors of the mode of performance and the outcome of complex cognitive tasks such as *decision-making*. Now, if it is truth that decision-making styles exist that the individuals use with the majority frequency of others, it is as truth that these styles are not rigid and immutable (Glaser and Weber 2005), but flexible and modifiable in answer to specific situations (Driver, Brousseau, Hunsaker 1990).

A decision-making strategy is a sequence of cognitive and conative mental operations (environmental actions) used to transform the initial state of knowledge into a final knowledge in which the decision maker considers the decision-making problem solved. The cognitive strategies are chosen on the grounds of a series of factors: the way in which the information is proposed, the complexity of the problem, the decision-making context and the characteristics of the decision maker (Hastie and Dawes 2001). These variables, regardless of the values of alternatives, influence the selection of strategies by modifying the cognitive effort needed to implement them (Bettman 1993). Empirical and theoretical research matured within the psychology of decision suggests that cognitive strategies follow pathways often different from those posed by *rational choice* economics. According to the model of the adaptive decision maker, developed by Payne, Bettman and Johnson (1993), decision-making is a highly contingent form of information processing by which individuals use adaptive and heuristic decision-making strategies as a response to the limited capacity of information processing and the complexity of decision-making tasks. A key feature of our cognitive system is the extraordinary flexibility of our decision-making strategies. First, in making a choice, individuals consider accuracy and cognitive effort not as absolute attributes associated with a strategy, but rather as dependent on a single situation. This assessment – which can be detected a priori (*top-down* mode) and during the same decision-making (*bottom-up* mode) – can influence the choice of the various decision making strategies available. The selected strategy will be the one that will allow taking a good decision with the least effort. Generally, the most frequent simplification strategies are commonly classified as compensatory and non-compensatory (Payne, Bettman and Johnson 1993). The first ones are based on a quantitative judgment and are implemented when the attributes describing the various decision-making alternatives are commensurable among themselves based on the attractiveness / utility values. In other words, an individual chooses an alternative that has an attribute such as to compensate for the sacrifice he is willing to perform without renouncing other appreciable attributes. Non-compensatory strategies, however, are used for those decision-making problems where options and criteria are immeasurable and the attractiveness of an option over a certain criterion, cannot be offset by the higher attractiveness of the same option compared to another criterion. It is often that individuals find themselves to mediate between accuracy and cognitive effort in selecting the most appropriate strategy for task requests: in this case, a certain flexibility is needed in using the strategies to be adopted. Decision-making, considered as a cognitive activity with limited capacity, seeks to meet multiple goals, such as minimizing emotional weight due to conflicting values between alternatives, reaching socially acceptable and justifiable decisions, making accurate decisions that maximize the benefits and minimize the cognitive effort to acquire and process the information (Hogart 1987). The latter is defined according to the amount of time and the type of mental operations required implementing a certain decision-making strategy. Zipf (1949) proposes the principle of the minimum cognitive effort, according to which a strategy is selected that ensures the minimum effort in achieving a specific desired result. Le strategie che comportano scelte più accurate sono spesso quelle che implicano più sforzo e ciò indica come la selezione delle strategie sia il risultato di un compromesso tra il desiderio di prendere la decisione più corretta e lo sforzo minore (Johnson and Payne 1985). The literature topic follow the distinction is made between compensatory and non-compensatory strategies.

Compensatory strategies

- *Additive Difference (ADD)*: this strategy is based on a comparison of two options at a time, attribute per attribute. Subsequently, the differences between the attributes are added in order to reach an overall evaluation of the two options (Tversky 1969). The best alternative is compared with the next option and so on. Finally, the option chosen is the one that surpasses all comparisons.
- *Equal Weights (EQW)*: this is a decision-making strategy based on the examination of all alternatives and all the values assigned to each alternative, ignoring the information about the importance or probability of each attribute (Dawes 1979). In other words, the final choice falls on the option with the highest overall utility score (i.e. the sum of the utilities of each option).

- *The Multi-Attribute Utility Model (MAU):* this is a normative rule that chooses the option with the main utility defined as the sum of the usefulness of the various attributes (Anderson 1974).
- *The Majority of Confirming Dimensions (MCD):* as in ADD, this strategy involves treating options pairs. The values of each of the two options are compared for each attribute. The option with the greatest quantity of winning attributes is compared by that one following (Russo and Dosher 1983). Such a comparison to couples ends only after having valued all the options and having identified that one winning.

Non-compensatory strategies

- *Disjunctive (DIS)* a product is evaluated in relation to what we believe is its best feature by neglecting everyone else.
- *Elimination-By-Aspects* (EBA): this strategy is based on the idea that, the decision maker did not evaluate decision-making alternatives, as such, but based on their characteristics (Tversky 1972). The first step is to select a single aspect and eliminate from alternatives all those that do not contemplate it. This deletion process ends only when there is only one option.
- *Lexicographic (LEX):* thanks to this strategy, the decider evaluates the options available only based on the most important feature. The final choice, therefore, falls to the option that this feature has the best value (Fishburn 1974). In the event that more than one option had the same value as the most important feature, the evaluation of the best alternatives would be based on the next important feature, and so on.
- *Recognition Heuristic (REC):* in some choices, especially in *real-world* contexts, people have so little information that they simply choose the alternative that is more familiar. In other words, the heuristics of recognition are often applied, often with success. This strategy can be considered as a particular case of LEX, with the difference that here the most important attribute is the recognition of the name (Goldstein and Gigerenzer 2002). If there are multiple options with the same value, the best value option for the second most important attribute is selected, and so on.
- *Satisficing Heuristic (SAT)/Conjunctive:* in this case, the decision-maker considers only one alternative at a time and compares the values of each of its attributes with a suction level or default threshold value. The alternative is chosen or refused; depending on what all his attributes present values to of above or under the esteemed threshold. The choice will fall on the most satisfactory

alternative in relation to all the esteemed attributes, that is that one that satisfies least prearranged standard.

- *Random*: this strategy, for which choice is made without consulting any available information, can be used in case of time pressure or high complexity of the task (Payne 1976). In general, individuals can adapt them, replace them, or combine them with a flexible use of strategies. In the case of a recombination of strategies there is an initial phase in which the weaker alternatives are eliminated and a second phase in which the remaining alternatives are examined in more detail.

Decision-making strategies, as is evident, do not have a logical structure. In most concrete situations, in fact, evaluating available alternatives is computationally unsustainable, influenced by prejudices, time, limited information, and more.

According to Lipshitz and Strauss (1997), which have conducted numerous studies on heuristic strategies by which individuals face uncertainty in "natural" contexts – in Kahneman's and Tversky's approach the standard methodology for dealing with uncertainties – which can be synthesized with the formula RQP heuristic (Reduce: reduce uncertainty through a thorough search of information; Quantify: quantify the uncertainty that cannot be reduced; Plug: inserting the result into a formal scheme that includes uncertainty as a factor in choosing a certain course of action) – is incomplete because it lacks the individual-environment *feedback* present in most decision-making situations (Klein 1998). Otherwise, studies conducted under Naturalistic Decision Making describe how decision makers face uncertainty without resorting to RQP calculations or heuristics. In other words, to cope with uncertainties, decision makers would use the following five coping strategies summarized in the RAWFS heuristic formula:

1. *Reduction*: it try to reduce uncertainty through searching for information.
2. *Assumption-based reasoning*: it tries to fill information gaps based on past knowledge or imagination.
3. *Weighing*: are valued pros and cons of the various options (an approximate version of the AU model).
4. *Forestalling*: provide for an action course to counteract any negative contingencies, for example, by building alternative action plans for the worst cases.
5. *Suppressing uncertainty*: for example, ignoring it or taking risky decisions.

Conclusions

Over the next few years, and with the increasingly accurate contribution of cognitive neuroscience, we may have further reflection on this difficult terrain. Certainly, however, we can now say that without highly performing decision-making devices such as those studied by the *Naturalistic Decision Making* paradigm, the construction of civilization, and possibly the same evolution of the species, would have been impossible. Perhaps it is not paradoxical to think that these have developed from the cognitive limitations of man, revealing themselves flexible in the face of unforeseen and above all ecological situations for the use of environmental resources (Maldonato and Dell'Orco 2010). In this sense, if it is truth that the human mind has accumulated information and knowledge by means of a prominent quantity of rational decisions, the enormous majority of the decisions has been supported by a natural logic whose rules have been shown naturally advantageous.

References

Anderson N.H. (1974) "Algebraic models of perception". In Carterette E.C., Friedman, M.P. (eds.), *Handbook of Perception* (vol. 2). Academic Press, New York.

Bettman J.R. (1993) "The decision maker who came in from the cold". In McAlister, L., Rothschild, M. (eds.), *Advances in Consumer Research*, 10, pp. 7–11.

Dawes R.M. (1979) "The robust beauty of improper linear models in decision making". In *American Psychologist*, 34, pp. 571–582.

Driver M.J., Brousseau K.R., Hunsaker P.L. (1990) *The Dynamic Decision Maker*. Harper and Row Publishers, New York.

Epstein S., Pacini R., Denes-Raj V., Heiner H. (1996) "Individual difference in intuitive-experiential and analytical-rational thinking styles". In *Journal of Personality and Social Psychology*, 71, pp. 390–405.

Fishburn P.C. (1974) "Lexicographic Orders, Utilities and Decision Rules: A Survey". In *Management Science*, 20 (11), pp. 1442–1471.

Gigerenzer G. (1997) *Bounded Rationality: Models of Fast and Frugal Inference*, Max Planck Institute for Human Development, Berlin.

Gigerenzer G. (2001) "The adaptive toolbox". In Gigerenzer, G., Selten, R. (eds.), *Bounded Rationality: The Adaptive Toolbox*. MIT Press, Cambridge, Mass.

Gigerenzer G. (2009) *Decisioni Intuitive*, Cortina, Milano.

Gigerenzer G., Goldstein D. G. (1996) "Reasoning the fast and frugal way: Models of bounded rationality". In *Psychological Review*, 103 (4), pp. 650–669.

Glaser M., Weber M. (2005) "Overconfidence and trading volume". In *Working Paper*, University of Mannheim.

Goldstein D.G., Gigerenzer G. (2002) "Models of ecological rationality: the recognition heuristic". In *Psychological Review*, 109 (1), pp. 75–90.

Hamilton D.L., Gifford R.K. (1976) "Illusory Correlation in Interpersonal Perception: A cognitive bases of stereotypic judgments". In *Journal of Experimental and Social Psychology*, 12 (4), pp. 136–149.

Hastie R., Dawes R.M. (2001) *Rational Choice in an Uncertain World: The Psychology of Judgment and Decision Making*, Sage, Thousand Oaks.

Hogart R.M. (1987) *Judgement and Choice: The psychology of decision*, Wiley, New York.

James, W. (1950) *The Principles of Psychology*, vol. II. New York: Dover Publications.

Johnson E.J., Payne J.W. (1985) "Effort and accuracy in choice". In *Management Science*, 31 (4), pp. 394–414.

Kagan J., Rosman B.L., Day D., Albert J., Phillips W. (1964) "Information processing in the child: significance of analytic and reflective attitudes". *Psychological Monographs*, 78, pp. 1–37

Kahneman D., Frederick S. (2002) "Representativeness revisited: Attribute substitution in intuitive judgment". In Gilovich T., Griffin D. and Kahneman D. (eds.), *Heuristics and Biases: The psychology of intuitive judgment*. Cambridge University Press, Cambridge.

Kahneman D., Slovic P., Tversky A. (1982) *Judgment under Uncertainty: Heuristics and biases*. Cambridge University Press, New York.

Kasparov G. (2008) *How Life Imitates Chess: Making the right moves, from the board to the boardroom*, Bloomsbury Publishing, USA.

Kaufmann G. (1979) "The Explorer and the Assimilator: a cognitive style distinction and its potential implications for innovative problem solving". In *Scandinavian Journal of Educational Research*, 23, 101–108.

Kirton M.J. (1976) "Adaptors and innovators, a description and measure". In *Journal of Applied Psychology*, 61, 622–629.

Klein G.A. (1993) "Recognition-primed decisions". In W. B. Rouse (ed.), *Advances in Man-Machine Systems Research*. JAI Press, Greenwich.

Klein G.A. (1998) *Sources of Power: How people make decisions*. MIT Press, Cambridge, Mass.

Klein G.A., Calderwood R. (1991) "Decision Model: some lessons from the field". In *IEEE Transactions on Systems Man and Cybernetics*, 21 (5), pp. 1018–1026.

Lipshitz R., Strauss O. (1997) "Coping with uncertainty: A naturalistic decision making analysis". In *Organizational Behavior and Human Decision Processes*, 69 (2), pp. 149–163.

Lipshitz R., Klein G., Orasanu J., Salas E. (2001) "Taking stock of Naturalistic Decision Making". In *Journal of Behavioral Decision Making*, 14 (5), pp. 331–352.

Loewenstein G. (2001) "The creative destruction of decision research". In *Journal of Consumer Research*, 28, pp. 499–505.

Maldonato M. (2010) *Decision Making: Towards an Evolutionary Psychology of Rationality*. Sussex Academic Press, Brighton; Portland; Toronto.

Maldonato M., Dell'Orco S. (2010) "Toward an Evolutionary Theory of Rationality". In *World Futures*, 66 (2), pp. 103–123.

March J. (1994) *A Primer on Decision making: How decisions happen.* The Free Press, New York.

Marschak J., Radner R. (1972) *Economic Theory of Teams.* Yale University press, New Haven.

Mullainathan S., Thaler R.H (2000) "Behavioral economics". In *National Bureau of Economic Research* (NBER), Working Paper 7948.

Nisbett R.E. e Ross L. (1980) *Human Inference: Strategies and shortcomings of social judgment.* Prentice-Hall, Englewood Cliffs.

Pask G. (1972) "A fresh look at cognition and the individual". *International Journal of Man-Machine Studies*, 4, pp. 211–216.

Payne J.W. (1976) "Task complexity and contingent processing in decision making: An information search and protocol analysis". In *Organizational Behavior and Human Performance*, 16, pp. 366–387.

Payne J.W., Bettman J.R., Johnson E.J. (1993) *The Adaptive Decision Maker.* Cambridge University Press, Cambridge.

Richardson R.C. (1998) "Heuristics and satisficing". In Bechtel W., Graham, G. (eds.), *A Companion to Cognitive Science.* Blackwell Publishers, Oxford.

Riding R.J., Glass A., Douglas G. (1993) "Individual differences in thinking: cognitive and neurophysiological perspectives". Special Issues: *Thinking. Educational Psychology*, 13 (3,4), pp. 267–279.

Russo J.E., Dosher B.A. (1983) "Strategies for multiattribute binary choice". In *Journal of Experimental Psychology: Learning, Memory, & Cognition*, 9, pp. 676–696.

Schwarz N., Vaughn L.A. (2002) "The availability heuristic revisited: Recalled content and ease of recall as information". In Gilovich T., Griffin D. and Kahneman D. (eds.), *The Psychology of Intuitive Judgment: Heuristics and biases.* Cambridge University Press, Cambridge, England.

Schwartz B., Ward A., Monterosso J., Lyubomirsky S., White K., Lehman D.R. (2002) "Maximizing versus satisficing: happiness is a matter of choice". In *Journal of Personality and Social Psychology*, 83 (5), pp. 1178–1197.

Scott S.G., Bruce R.A. (1995) "Decision making style: the development of a new measure". In *Educational and Psychological Measurement*, 55, pp. 818–831.

Selten R. (1998) "Aspiration adaptation theory". In *Journal of Mathematical Psychology*, 42, pp. 191–214.

Simon H.A. (1997) *Models of Bounded Rationality*, vol. 3. MIT Press, Boston.

Simon H.A. (1979) "Rational decision making in business organizations" (Nobel Lecture, Stockholm, 1978). In *American Economic Review*, 69, pp. 493–512.

Simon H. S. (1983) *Reason in Human Affairs.* Stanford University Press, Stanford, California.

Stanovich K.E. (1999) *Who is rational? Studies of individual differences in reasoning.* Erlbaum, Hillsdale.

Stanovich K.E., West R.F. (1998) "Individual differences in reasoning: Implications for the rationality debate". In *Behavioral and Brain Sciences*, 23, pp. 645–665.

Stigler G. (1961) "The economics of information". In *Journal of Political Economy*, 69, pp. 213–25.

Tietz R. (1992) "Semi-normative theories based on bounded rationality". In *Journal of Economic Psychology*, 13 (2), pp. 297–314.

Todd P.M., Gigerenzer G. (2000) "Précis of simple heuristics that make us smart". In *Behavioral and Brain Sciences*, 23 (5), pp. 727–780.

Tversky A. (1969) "Intransitivity of preferences". In *Psychological Review*, 76 (1), pp. 31–48.

Tversky A. (1972) "Elimination by aspects: A Theory of Choice". In *Psychological Review*, 79 (4), pp. 281–299.

Witkin H.A. (1962) *Psychological Differentiation: Studies of Development*. Wiley, New York.

Zipf G.K. (1949) *Human Behavior and the Principle of Least Effort*. Addison Wesley Press, Cambridge, MA.

2

Decision-making and Personality in Clinical Psychology

RAFFAELE SPERANDEO, DANIELA IENNACO,
NELSON MAURO MALDONATO, SILVIA DELL'ORCO

Dimensional Theories of Personality and Decision-making Styles

The current revision of the concept of personality disorder proposed by Section III of DSM 5 assimilates the pathology to the normal functioning of personality by interpreting the first as an extreme variant of the ordinary process of adapting an individual to his environment.

At the origin of this innovative reading, which abandons the concept of diagnostic category, there is the awareness that the affective and emotional valences of the individual represents the distinctive feature of his being in the world and the way he does and interprets his choices, and the ordinary decisions of own existence.

Emotion can be define as a chain of events between the appearance of an environmental stimulus and response behavior; it manifests itself on multiple levels: psychological, physiological and behavioral. Emotion drives our choices, resulting a decisive factor in decision-making. Even though humans prefer to emphasize their rationality, their nature remains eminently emotional and affective. Emotions and feelings are, in fact, our main connection with things and people, and experiences shape us through emotions, before with facts or with reasoning about them.

In this respect, the last two decades have witnessed a true revolution in the field of science. In fact, many scientists and psychologists currently assume that emotions, good or bad, are the main guideline for the most significant decisions in life. The recent and growing attention of the scientific world to emotions is because individuals are not move in their choices only by rational factors or economic interest.

The personality disorder and theorized in the DSM 5 Section III proposal as a dysfunctional process that concern primarily the affective and emotional areas: empathy, identity, self-directedness and intimacy. In this sense, the pathological personality is not qualitatively different from the "normal" personality and the expressive rigidity of the pathological character traits can be conceptualized as a special condition, in which a behavioral style, otherwise normal, stiffens in relation to an environmental context, that puts the decision making modes of that particular personality style into crisis. For example, an avoidant character structure is adaptive, where the hostile environment favours cautious and circumspect behaviors and becomes pathological in contexts where continuous and rapid relational opening is required. The area of the identity of these subjects, which rests on a delicate balance between self-evaluation and judgment of others, changes in relation to the impossibility of modifying the exposure to judgment and causes a stiff withdrawal from the relationships. This process is obviously affective and emotional. The types of personalities classified as pathological are therefore a valid way to investigate the normal character of which express the typical decision-making and relational modes in an accentuated manner. Over the past twenty years, the study of emotions has resurfaced. New trends in research have highlighted the emotional root of human behavior. Emotions, passions, feelings and affections they have shown themselves as the deep matrices of culture, indeed the pillars on which they be based. This peripheral and partial sector has become increasingly central and dominant. *Homo sentiens o patiens* are before of the *homo sapiens o faber*, connected to passions and emotions, without which neither the *ratio* nor the *actio* structure, are defined and realized because they involve choices, values guidelines and subjective dispositions (Cambi 1998).

Studies that deal with emotions and decisions have doubled since 2004. Emotion and decision making go hand in hand. (Coughlan and Connolly 2001, Mellers 2000), but despite this scientific evidence, it is important to bear in mind that the field of study is still young and that although the theories of reference to understand how and with what intensity the emotions affect decision-making, exist and are increasing, they are not exhaustive.

What happens in our mind when we are facing two conflicting options, either attractive or unpleasant? The choices between two conflicting options can be seen as the channel through which emotion drives you every day trying to avoid negative feelings (guilt, regret) and increase positive ones (pride and happiness). Lewin is the author who first systematically theorized the concept of choice. According to Lewin, one must imagine the individual as engaged in an attempt to find a definitive answer to his uncertainty, as if he were at the centre of a field attracted by forces of equal intensity. When this happens, the man is confronted with a conflict, that is, two tendencies both appealing but of different origin: they both attract it, but the direction of the "*I like*" may be contrary to "*I want*". While some theoretical models seem to suggest that the dimension of "*I like*" prevails over the rational budget, it also seems undeniable that man has the ability to act against his emotional desires in view of a deeper need of his own personality. While it is true that emotions direct our choices, it is also true that making an assertive choice requires subordination (not elimination) of emotion / affectivity to rationality.

Interest in emotions has led to substantial criticism of one of the strong conceptions of Western thought: the dichotomy of emotion-reason (Cattarinussi 2013). In fact, in a vision of the human being as incarnate and enacted mind, such dichotomy has no reason to exist; emotions and reason must be, rather understood as arranged along the continuum of the process of adaptation to the environment.

In such sense, the study of the pathological behavioral types fits in the discussion still opened among the weight of the emotionality or the rationality in the determination of the choices. The proposal emerging from this survey is oriented at considering decision styles and adaptation processes as a function of the typology of character. It is easy to perceive how any personality disorder be describe as a decision style determined by specific affective rigidities.

Obsessive style presupposes a marked difficulty in managing intimacy due to the impact of anger and anxiety have on this area. This results in rigidly moral, rational and perfectionist style.

The borderline structure presupposes a difficulty in the area of self-determination based on the prevalence of aggressive emotions and the identity area due to lack of basic security. This results in an impulsive and unstable decision-making style.

Depending style presupposes a shortage of identity and self-direction-ality based on low self-esteem. This results in a decision style strictly adhering to the guidelines of the cultural reference system.

The narcissistic and antisocial style presupposes a deficit of empathy and intimacy, based on a shortage of the intensity and emotional experi-ence, which with different gravity express themselves in egoistic and prevaricators attitudes. This results in a rigid and unmodifiable decision style.

The schizoid and paranoid style presupposes a deficit of all four affec-tive dimensions in the game, determined by a difficulty accessing all the emotional experiences, also minimal, that express themselves in relational retirement and in a poor and incoherent decision style.

The Categorical Models of Personality Disorders and the Ability to Self-determination

In the classical definition of the American Psychiatric Association manuals, the concept of Personality refers to stable patterns of thoughts, emotions, motivations and behaviors that are ordinarily and consistently, activated by an individual in his interaction with the environment aimed at continually seeking an optimal adjustment (Oldham, Skodol, Bender 2017). This definition is a reductive, but definitely has the advantage to highlight two important aspects of the current idea of personality its dynamic nature (personality changes through a continuous interaction between the subject and the environment) and flexibility. Starting from this personality definition, the latest psychiatric texts agree that personality disorders only occur when such patterns is expressed in extreme and destructive manner and limit the subject and the environment. These inflexible and inadequate behavioral traits create difficulties in adaptation and malaise.

Specifically, DSM 5 (2014) indicates that a personality disorder is a constant pattern of inner experience and of the behavior that deviates sharply from the expectations of the individual's culture, is pervasive and inflexible, begins in adolescence or early adulthood, is stable over time and causes disablement or uneasiness. It implies a widespread disorganization in the personality structure and the functioning of the subject that is manifested by a marked failure in the development of important personality and capacity structures necessary for an adaptive operation of the subject.

The presence of a Personality Disorder, according to DSM 5, is due to the lack of a stable and consistent sense of self and chronic dysfunction in interpersonal relationships.

The World Health Organization in its ICD-10 (International Classification of Diseases) uses in the F. 60/69 a similar classification:

These types of condition include deeply ingrained and enduring behavior patterns, manifesting as inflexible responses to a broad range of personal and social situations. They represent extreme or significant deviations from the way in which the average individual in a given culture perceives, thinks, feels and, particularly, relates to others. Such behavior patterns tend to be stable and to encompass multiple domains of behavior and psychological functioning.

They are frequently, but not always, associated with various degrees of subjective distress and problems of social performance.

If personality, therefore, is the set of permanent traits, which include the ways in which a person is inclined to think, feel and act, personality disorder occurs when all traits are maladaptive and causes personal and relational suffering and a clinically and relevant discomfort in a social and work related contexts. In a person who has a personality disorder the ways in which he is inclined to think, feel, act, directly or indirectly, undermine his adaptive functioning. The diagnosis of PD (Parkinson's disease) also requires that these traits are stable, pervasive, difficult to control or modify, and markedly different from the expectations of the culture of belonging.

In this regard, it should be emphasized that although even healthy subjects often express extreme expressions of their character traits that lead them to think, feel, and act in order to harm themselves, this is not enough to diagnose a personality disorder. Such diagnosis requires dysfunctional traits to be stable, pervasive, difficult to control and / or modify, and markedly different from the expectations of the reference culture.

Regarding the etiology, personality disorders seem determined by the interaction between genetic factors that seem to create the right soil to the impact of unfavourable and adverse environmental conditions (Paris 2001).

As far as it concerns the aetiology, the personality troubles seem determined by the interaction between genetic factors, which seem to create the ground fit for the impact of unfavourable and adverse environmental conditions (Jang and Vernon 2001).

Adverse environmental determinants seem to play a more significant role and include:

1. Family problems such as brutal separations, sudden or traumatic deaths, severe psychopathological conditions of parents;
2. Childish traumatic experiences such as sexual, emotional and physical abuse or carelessness;
3. Stressful social factors such as war, poverty and migration.

This vision of personality disorders is suitable for approaching the analysis of capacity of free self-determination in relation to the emergence of pathology of and of the auto and hetero aggressive violent behaviors.

Personality disorders are closely associated with severely pathological behaviors such as self-harm, suicide and violence against others. A study that has used personality disorder classification DSM (Diagnostic and Statistical Manual of mental disorders) has shown that people with a Cluster B disorder have a 10 times higher probability of having a criminal conviction and a 8 times higher probability of spending time in prison (Coid *et al.* 2006). Self-harm has been predominantly associated with childhood sexual abuse; while, hetero directed violence has been connected whit childhood physical abuse (Waxman *et al.* 2014).

People with a personality disorder have behind, usually, stories of psycho-social and economic discomfort; have been victims of trauma, negligence and abuse in childhood, from adults lead chaotic, fragmented and desperate lives, suffering high levels of psychological discomfort and social marginalization.

Self-harm, suicide and heterodirect violence can arise in disparate situations, but in the case of personality disorders, they seem to be a maladaptive coping mechanism. In this sense, these pathological phenomena have, in clinical terms, specific functions.

Heterodirect violence, for example, has purposes that are easy to understand from our cultural perspective. In addition to the purpose of obtaining material goods, it may serve for the following purposes:

1. Emotional regulation; when it expresses impulsive liberation and the expression of strong emotions such as rage.
2. Social and interpersonal dominance; when mature in accordance with the cultural stereotype of masculinity.
3. Revenge; when expressing retaliation or compensation towards who have committed wrongdoing or caused damages.
4. Protection (Defence) from Future Damage: When acting as a deterrent to those who threaten future damage.

Like all behaviors that efficiently fulfil various functions, violence can become an effective habit of achieving conscious and unconscious goals.

Heterodirect violence has roots in the infantile experiences of Interfamilial violence or the wider social context in which there have been few opportunities to learn alternative ways of dealing with anger and other emotions (Blair, Mitchell and Blair 2005; Howells 2009, Raine 2013).

In fact, violence can be part of the fabric of a community where it is accepted and even anticipated as necessary for success and survival. Violent behavior can serve people with a personality disorder as a means of establishing control when they feel a threat to their physical and psychological well-being, including the potential shame feeling of those who have been victims in the past or they are undergo to topical mistreatments.

With regard to self-directed violence, in our cultural perspective it is much more difficult to understand the reasons behind it, because we think that people naturally tend to avoid hurting themselves. However, people who practice self-harm act to hurt themselves. Therefore, we may consider self-harm as the expression of a basic pathology, unless we understand the coping functions that this behavior subtend. In the context of personality disorders, psychopathological exploration and patient stories reveal that self-harm serves for six different purposes:

1. Act on the emotional self-relation: people with a PD live a strong emotional discomfort and self-harm can provide them with an effective means of controlling rage, shame that can be particularly strong in those who come from backgrounds with psychosocial and economic discomfort and who have suffered childhood neglect and mistreatments. It can offer relief in various ways: distracting from emotional pain, replacing it with the physical one and / or with the release of endorphins; providing a way of expressing, releasing and acting anger and aggression just like in heterodirect violence; or conversely, allowing people to feel something different from emotional and paralysing dissociation. In other words, self-harm is a mechanism of control that can provide relief from a negative emotional experience.

2. Self-punishment: people with a PD usually have low self-esteem, believe they are bad, and deserve punishments. Self-harm can be the expression of this, especially in the face of strong emotions such as rage and shame.

3. Communication: Self-harm can be a way of communicating a strong emotional suffering by symbolizing emotions in a concrete mode, in physical form "public expression of a private punishment" (Adshead 1997, p. 11).

4. Punishment of the Other: It is normal to experience aggression and anger towards those who have hurt us or those we take care; self-harm is a sure way of expressing anger when heterodirect rage is considered unacceptable. Self-harm correlates with the experience of being attached that it generates in the other self-harm; so it becomes a symbolic weapon that moves anger to others on itself, even though it communicates it.

5. Control: self-harm can generate a sense of power and control by re-establishing property on own body in the face of the experience of being victims. This may be particularly relevant to those who have suffered physical or sexual abuse during childhood. The background of the persons whose bodies have been violated, can be interpreted, then, be like an act of claim of the own body, that

like an identification mechanism with the executioner (Freud 1992).

6. Continuum with suicide: When accompanied by a personality disorder, the desire to kill is an expression of desperation and of permanent escape from the sufferings of life. On the contrary, self-harm offers short-term relief and can be seen as an act of hope, as Anna Motz (2009) claims, a statement of life.

Relate the extreme anger, the anxiety, and the shame that can undergo self-harm to adverse and traumatic backgrounds, typical of personality disorders. In this self-harm context as a coping tool, it makes us understand why people find relief from negative emotional experience. To the extent that self-harm effectively performs this function can become a habit.

On these analyses, you can set up a first description of the decision-making functions of subjects with personality disorders. It is evident from the above that it is not possible to trace a clear line between self-directed violence understood as a pathology, and a heterodirect intent as an intentional act of criminal nature. Both pathological behaviors underpin instrumental value and serve for purposes that are evidently oriented to maintaining the psychic balance of the subject. However, self-directed violence does not imply the will to harm others and this could indicate an attitude of morality and respect for the law.

According to our cultural perspective, violence, on many occasions, is seen as a choice and is subjective to some degree of control. Generally, people are able to choose not to act violently and stop the flow of action.

The evidence of this presumption is clear: when it is sufficiently motivated to give up violence (self-directed or heterodirect) in a variety of contexts, people do it. Consider, for example, an irascible man who is systematically involved in conflict and resorts to violence; often this mode stops at the sight of a police officer. On this occasion, he is strongly motivated not to explode his aggression not be arrested and accused of aggression. This mental experiment of the "Police officer behind" shows that the individual has the ability to choose not to be violent and to control his aggressiveness, a skill he certainly exercises, only when he is sufficiently motivated. These types of "behind" tests also exist for self-directed violence as when a person who is regularly self-injury, to be certain that his children do not see him, hangs in their presence. The violent behavior that responds to coping needs, so it seems to be subject to a choice and some degree of control. Exercising this ability seems to be generally something people can do, but they do not. Nonetheless, it is extremely important to recognize how difficult it can be for people with personality disorder to abstain from violence, especially when it is habitual and serves to achieve an emotional balance that people cannot reach by other means.

To the extent that violence offers the adjustment of affections, abstinence requires the person to endure the underlying feelings of shame and extreme anger at least until and until alternative coping tools are learned. In other words, if they choose to abstain from violence they may be subject to some form of internal constriction.

The presumption that violence is subject to choice and to some degree of control can be excluded in particular circumstances. Perhaps, the people easily irritable become so angry that something explodes and choice and control are lost, making them able to stop the flow of violent behavior. Regard to the control ability, to understand if the violent persons with diagnosis of trouble of personality can auto-determine their behaviour, it is necessary to regard two important aspects. The first concerns the nature of the desires and the principles that the person pursues in the deliberative process. The second is the underlying emotional suffering.

A wide agreement exists inside the pertinent literature (Buchanan and Brock 1989), the subjects that can choose on deliberate way, pursue wishes and stable and lasting objectives. It is possible then to assume consciously decisions that have heavy consequences, unjustified in appearances, or that go against the own interests, if these decisions are not based on a whim but they are adopted coherently with wishes, interests, stable values and objectives well organised

Subjects with personality disorders lack the capacity to represent themselves in a harmonious and integrated way and often make choices without reference to values dimensions, stable and coherent. Their determinations, often, is based on "acting out", i.e. actions carried out under the impulse of uncontrollable impulses.

When the decision lacks this character of consistency with the range of desires, values, and goals, emotional control and self-determination capability, is not fully satisfied, and therefore it is legitimate to question the integrity of the subject's the capacity to understand and discern.

Since all subjects with personality, disorders present an impairment of the "self" as impairment of the ability to self-rationality, intimacy, identity and empathy (DSM 5, SEZ III). Scrupulous assessment is required on a case-by-case basis of the magnitude of this compromise that when it exceeds a certain limit does not allow the subject to adhere coherently to the shared values of the social and cultural micro-group.

The second aspect that can undermine the ability to understand and desire is the fact that people with a personality disorder who want to self-harm or attack others, experience great emotional suffering. The clinical context presume people with a personality disorder to be capable of understanding and wanting even if emotionally sufferer. Despite this presumption, it should be considered that emotional suffering, however, destroys the ability to make autonomous decisions and the available diagnostic tools do not value this accurately. Such concern can arise in part because the prevailing cultural conception is that emotions interfere with reasoning and rationality.

Sometimes emotions can blind our abilities to decide, the great emotional suffering experienced by those with a personality disorder, that is aggressive towards others or who tries suicide makes them unable to see future happiness opportunities. Conversely, an accurate assessment would add hope and treatment could help them see possible life alternatives.

Conclusions

From this brief overview of the dimensional and categorical models of personality and its disorders, three deserving elements of reflection and scientific deepening emerge. The first concerns dichotomy between emotions and rationality in the process of adaptation to the environment and decision-making. Although rationality seems to us the best way to adapt to the environment and to choose the most convenient for our social and relational functioning, it is evident that the ability to handle emotions discriminates between the various character styles and thus among the various ways to make choices. In fact, even a rigidly rational decision-making style that appears be linked to the obsessive character structure is actually determined by the need to keep anger and anxiety under control and expresses a defect in managing these painful emotions that is compensated by a rigid rational modality.

The second element concerns the relationship between pathology and self-determination, which in its more refined expressions appears, rooted in the ability to adhere in stable and coherently manner to a shared or understandable value system. When empathic capacity and self-directionality are deficient, the choices be made, based on the impulse determined by occasional states. In these situations, the ability of self-determination of the subject can be consider markedly compromised.

The third element concerns the impact of emotional suffering on the ability to decide appropriately on their own needs. This strictly psychopathological aspect connotes the decision-making ability in its clinical side and clarifies the borderline dimension of personality pathologies. These pathologies present a characteristic of the adequacy of reality examination based on the integrity of cognitive functions. Unlike psychoses, they appear be safeguarded and they do not always guarantee the correctness of the choices of subjects affected by these disorders that under the thrust of emotional suffering may give up any form of organized action that is consistent with reality.

References

Adshead G. (1997) *Written on the body: Deliberate self-harm and violence. A Practical Guide to Forensic Psychotherapy*. Jessica Kingsley Publishers, London.

American Psychiatric Association, Biondi M., Bersani F. S. (2014) *Manuale diagnostico e statistico dei disturbi mentali DSM-V*. Raffaello Cortina, Milano.

Blair J., Mitchell D., Blair K. (2005) *The Psychopath: emotion and the Brain*. Blackwell Publishing.

Buchanan A. E., Brock D. W. (1989) *Deciding for others: The ethics of surrogate decision making*. Cambridge University Press, Cambridge.

Cambi F. (1998) Nel conflitto delle emozioni. Prospettive pedagogiche. Armando Editore, Roma.

Cattarinussi B. (2013) Il gioco d'azzardo patologico. Non posso farne a meno. Aspetti sociali delle dipendenze. Franco Angeli, Milano.

Coughlan R., Connolly T. (2001) "Predicting affective responses to unexpected outcomes". In *Organizational Behavior and Human Decision Processes*, 85(2), pp. 211–225.

Farrington D. P., Coid J. W., Harnett L., Jolliffe D., Soteriou N., Turner R., West D. J. (2006) "Criminal careers up to age 50 and life success up to age 48: New findings from the Cambridge Study in Delinquent Development". In *Home Office Research Study*, 299.

Freud A. (1992) *The ego and the mechanisms of defence*. Karnac Books, London.

Howells K. (2009) "Recent developments and future directions in understanding cognition and emotion in offenders: a commentary". *Psychology, Crime & Law*, 15(2–3), pp. 285–292.

Jang K. L., Vernon P. A., Livesley W. J. (2001) "Behavioural-genetic perspectives on personality function". *The Canadian Journal of Psychiatry*, 46(3), pp. 234–244.

Mellers B. A. (2000) "Choice and the relative pleasure of consequences". In *Psychological Bulletin*, 126(6), p. 910.

Motz A. (2009) *Managing self-harm: Psychological Perspectives*. Routledge, London and New York

Paris J., Zweig-Frank H. (2001) "A 27-year follow-up of patients with borderline personality disorder". *Comprehensive psychiatry*, 42(6), pp. 482–487.

Raine A. (2013) *The anatomy of violence: The biological roots of crime*. Vintage, New York

Skodol A. E., Gunderson J. G., Shea M. T., McGlashan T. H., Morey L. C., Sanislow C. A., Pagano M. E. (2005) "The collaborative longitudinal personality disorders study (CLPS): Overview and implications". In *Journal of Personality Disorders*, 19(5), pp. 487–504.

Waxman R., Fenton M. C., Skodol A. E., Grant B. F., Hasin D. (2014) "Childhood maltreatment and personality disorders in the USA: Specificity of effects and the impact of gender". In *Personality and Mental Health*, 8(1), pp. 30–41.

Zeelenberg M. (1999) "Anticipated regret, expected feedback and behavioral decision making". *Journal of Behavioral Decision Making*, 12(2), p. 93.

3

Decision and Free Will between Psychology and Law

LUCA BARTOLI, NELSON MAURO MALDONATO,
RAFFAELE SPERANDEO

The purpose of this paper will be to describe how the term "will" has undergone profound transformation in the field of psychological and legal sciences, enriching itself, away, which the neuroscience and human sciences progressed in their research, content and meanings. We will also try to highlight the unresolved issues that remain when the concept of "will" finds its application in the legal sciences.

The Encyclopaedia Treccani defines the will "Power in man to choose and to achieve a suitable behavior for the attainment of certain ends". The will in ancient times constitutes one of the main philosophical problems, especially in its relation to reason. In Greek thought, the will is subordinate to reason and closely dependent on knowledge. With the advent of psychology, the concept of will be outlined in different ways in different schools, now as an autonomous function, which cannot be attributed to other psychic processes, now as a particularly differentiated form of instinctive-affective processes involving also the intellectual functions.

From a phenomenological point of view, the process of will is an autonomous, original process, irreducible to others. Who decides is aware of his decision; the processes of will not be reduced to cognitive or affective processes; you have real and elementary acts of will. Representations, feelings of tension, feelings of pleasure or disgust can or may not accompany these acts of will, but their presence is not necessary for volunteering. Jaspers thus differentiates the will from instinctive actions: "Primary impulses, instinctual motions, the representations of the purpose, end up mutually struggling as motives. From the comparison of these motives, as such appear as material, after the weighting, the oscillation and the struggle, be made the decision "I want" or "I do not want". This consciousness of free will is, alongside the experience of instinctual motions and alongside the experience of split personality, or the contraposition, an irreducible phenomenon. Only when a choice and a decision have been somehow lived, we speak of will, to act voluntarily".

We find ultimately the most interesting phenomenon, the constant and unique characteristic of the voluntary act: the consciousness of action. There are no suitable expressions to express this feeling; the subject is a simple spectator; everything be limited to a state of consciousness that the subject expresses as follows: "I am conscious of this choice", but in every description finds something escapes him, which he cannot do without distorting it. This perception of activity could be called the phenomenological form of the voluntary act. The characteristic of the elementary act of will is to be an inner activity and precisely a self-activity of the ego. It is good to add that this activity not be confused with the statement "I want", it is instead the orientation of the individual towards one purpose; it does not have to refer to the realization of something in the future, as to be an activity that is realized at present moment; it is the spontaneity of the ego that tilts and tends towards a purpose. While into the will, man has the consciousness of himself, as a conscious and unitary centre of a subjective activity directed towards a goal, in affective life, man reacts to the stimuli that act upon him. In the first case, the conscious self is affirmed; in the second case is the activity of the subject that participates, as with a resonance, in the life of the world around it. Only while in the affective life, the profound ego is involved into action, whose manifestations may also be above the limits of consciousness, but in voluntary action is the ego in the fullness of aware conscious that comes into play. On the will, they also influence the cognitive processes; the action of intelligence on the will is especially evident in choosing between the various motives that solicit our voluntary decision; intelligence shows us the meaning of various reasons that come to us as values and we make the choice based on a judgement.

To judge whether a man is responsible for an action, in case it is attributed to him, as his own, we must determine how, when preparing it, in the maturation of it, in implement it, his personality manifested himself. We can, therefore, from a psychological point of view, in everyday practice, hold to be that a man is responsible and to attribute an action as his own, as not because it is the result of a voluntary decision, because it is difficult to determine the mechanism of action of this decision, but as it manifests and reveals itself as a characteristic of a personality that in its will has its decisive and discriminative factor.

The concept of will is intimately linked to action: the will is act; the volition is the passage to the act. Reducing, as someone did, the volition to the simple resolution, that is, a theoretical statement that one thing will be done, is to build an abstraction. The choice is just a moment of the voluntary process. If it does not translate immediately or in good time, it does not distinguish itself from a logical operation of the spirit. Of course, in the term "action", we do not give the restricted meaning of movement, of act in the purely positive sense, but of a wider meaning: the meaning of "strong-willed manifestation". In fact, it is clear that strong-willed manifestation can consist not only of action in the strict sense, but also in the omission, that is, in a voluntary inert behavior. Not to mention, on the other hand, that volitional energy cannot be only externally but also internally, such as, for example, in the concentration of attention. We could then define the will as the process for which the subject acts by choosing between two or more different representations. Already in the Anglo-Saxon law of the nineteenth century, J.L. Austin introduced the theory of volitions, according to which human action was make up of two fundamental elements: the muscular movement that constitutes its beginning and the volition, that is, the state of mind that precedes and causes the movement.

Will is not a psychic state, but is a process that takes place in a conscious game of forces; it has a dynamic character, consumes and governs the energies. The essential aspect of the will is the subjective sentiment of the activity, or also the tension that accompanies each voluntary process. Only where choice and decision-making live, we can talk about voluntary process, this happens more often when our tension is greater. The essential one, in the strong-willed process, is the conscience of the activity. We have not an explanation about this. Attributing this force only to the voluntary act and the decision would be wrong; it is also presumable in instinctive impulses.

One can understand that the concept of choice between two or more options is implied in the term "will", is translated into English with the term "decision making" as it is a decision-making process. Some recent studies, carried out in particular, comparing the outcome of the neuropsychology test Iowa Gambling Task of healthy subjects vs. subjects with degenerative diseases of the central nervous system have highlighted the central role of specific brain structures in this decision-making process. In particular, the quality of decision-making was evaluated in subjects with multiple sclerosis (chronic inflammatory disease of the Central Nervous System characterized by demyelination (rather, loss of the sheath that envelops the part of the neuronal cell called axon resulting in altered signal transmission of the nervous system and symptoms sensorimotor) and the loss of grey substance (resulting in cognitive symptoms) versus healthy subjects, used as a control. The results obtained have substantially confirmed the role and complex interrelationship between the different brain structures already highlighted by functional neuroimaging studies, such as the dorsolateral prefrontal cortex (DLPFC); responsible for accumulation of information, the anterior cingulate cortex (ACC); implied in the attribution of importance in the possible reward resulting from the prediction of a stimulus, the orbital frontal cortex (OFC) for weighting a significant stimulus. Similarly, scientific studies focusing on possible genetic factors affecting abnormal behavior have yielded considerable results, so that some authors find it reasonable to believe that about 30% of antisocial behaviors can originate in genetic factors. In particular, the attention of researchers focused on the ability to identify specific genes implicated in the predisposition to different behavioral abnormalities. Specifically, brain-derived neurotrophic factor (BDNF) genes, those regulating the production of the nerve cell adhesion molecule (NCAM) and the serotonin transporter (5HTT) have been studied (Raine 2008). The researchers found out than the males of a family strain, who had aggressive behavior accompanied by mild mental retardation, had in the DNA mapping a multiform mutation (point mutation 6) in the gene encoding for the monoamine oxidase A (MAOA) neurotransmitter. This alteration causes the production of a shorter and not functioning protein. Males with this mutation exhibit abnormal levels of MAO-A in the urine (and presumably in the brain) where women of the same family strain, but with a single copy of that mutant gene, did not manifest this behavioral abnormality.

Benjamin Libet and colleagues (Libet et al. 1983) provided a decisive contribution to the discussion of the relationship between decision-making and motor activity. From the neurophysiological experimentation to establish with precision the moment in which the conscious decision to act is born, it results that brain activity begins before the subject is aware of that decision to act. Libet designed a tool that allowed the subject to experiment to have some autonomy in deciding when to make a response. The researcher recorded through the electroencephalograph the brain activity of the experimental subjects placed in front of a clock with a very fast pointer placed on a quadrant indicating the fractions of the second. He had therefore asked them to move their right hand at any time they chose, while simultaneously trying to keep track of the position of the hand on the dial at the instant they had deliberately decided to act. Libet had thus identified a temporal gap between the "readiness potential" on the EEGraphic tracing and the next instant of the decision referred by the subject. In turn, the consciousness of action precedes the real movement of several hundred milliseconds. In a document published in 2001, Libet summarizes his conclusions:

My conclusion about free will, one genuinely free in the non-deter-
mined sense, is then that its existence is at least as good, if not a
better, scientific option than is its denial by determinist theory.
Given the speculative nature of both determinist and non-deter-
minist theories, why not adopt the view that we do have free will
(until some real contradictory evidence may appear, if it ever does).
(Libet 2009, p. 156)

Recent experiments have shown that by studying the activity of a
specific frontal lobe area, it is possible to predict the outcome of a subject's
choice to move alternately the right and left hands a few seconds before
it becomes conscious.

However, you can highlight a critical observation: the execution mode
of the experiment measures when moving and not moving. Roskies
emphasized that the method used requires that the participants in the
experiment be at the same time alerted to an external signal (clock) and
to an internal signal (intent on making a move) and this could be interference in the information process. Finally, what is measured is not
conscious intention, but the consciousness of this conscious intention,
which is therefore very different. Libet's conclusions gave rise to some
criticism: considering that, he asked patients to tell him when they
decided to move his arm, apparently believing that conscience was necessary to give intentionality and personality to such an insignificant action.
In fact, he had only shown that informed decision-making takes time and
therefore it is not reasonable to think of the existence of a decision, a
choice or a conscious deliberation that systematically appears a moment
before any voluntary action, determining it. However, renouncing this
belief does not mean necessarily give up the idea that the voluntary
actions be relate to the person, the will, and conscience.

One should also consider the influence they may have on decision-
making, elements that seem to be irrelevant, such as the use of a foreign
language in communication. That choice be influenced by the context in
which it be made, so that it can feel the effect of prominence given by the
advantages rather than the disadvantages of a particular choice. In such
cases, language takes the value of a mean of providing information and /
or directing the attention of those who listen on specific features of the
decision. There are numerous studies suggesting that where the content
of an information is the same, the decision depends on whether the information itself is provided in the mother tongue or in a foreign language,
where the results of the experiments suggest that the risk appears more
contained if the information is provided in a foreign language. For
example, when people consider the danger inherent in certain activities,
such as traveling by air and the use of biotechnology, perceive the risk

associated with such lesser benefits if the information is transmitted in a foreign language In essence, new developments in the study of genetics and neuroscience have contributed to a better understanding of how interaction between genes and the environment, affects both the structure and functioning of our brain and our decision-making abilities, suggesting that biological determinism could play much greater role than it does not believe.

The concept of will therefore appears intimately connected with that of "freedom"; because of that, some Authors have identified the "free will" with the capacity of man, to form "second-order volitions". However, according to Frankfurt, one not be confused the freedom to act according to his own desires (qualities possessed by any animal capable of implementing the motives of his own motivational apparatus, with the freedom of will, a characteristic of man, who wants to direct his will in a way rather than in another). There is still an open debate in the philosophical field as well as in the psychology of the opportunity to consider a "free" act. Different aspects assume such significance, such as a) previous intention, (b) conscious thinking related to action, (c) prior deliberation to that effect, (d) a significant choice, (e) different effects of the action, and (f) the presence of a significant time interval between intent and action.

When judging the "degree of freedom" in an action of a subject, the nature of the action could play a significant role. For example, the action of grabbing a glass of water for drinking reflects an evolutionary action aimed at reintegrating basic physiological homeostasis. The freedom degree, in a necessary action from the biological point of view, it might be considered well diverged by when an action has instead optional characteristics, like the reading of a book.

The will takes on legal relevance with reference to the parties' ability to act, the classification of legal acts (i.e. acts of relevance governed by the legal system) and the defects of the will in legal acts. Right incorporates concepts of mind theory: for several centuries, moral and legal systems have, with some cultural and historical variations, included concepts such as intent, motive, and prediction. It is also certain that the inference of mental states in the evaluation of the action is one of the foundations of the legislative corpus; at the same time, however, the role of mental states in the legal decision-making process has often generated much doubt and controversy. At least two controversies can be traced in order to reach a fair and correct definition of mental states in the legal sphere: one has a conceptual value and is related to the precise use of mental state concepts in reasoning about the subject's actions and the consequent assignment of responsibility, guilt and punishment; the second assumes inferential character and consists in putting the reliable and accurate illations in the sections of mental states, starting from behavior and evidence related to the circumstances in which the action was taken. Moral responsibility depends crucially on the mental state with which a person acts. The assessment of mental states is therefore fundamental to the assessment of guilt in criminal law. Unlike traditional clinical assessments that usually relate to current functioning, forensic evaluations focus on the respondent's supposed actions and mental states (cognitive and / or voluntary) that may take days, weeks, months, and in some cases, years earlier. The forensic expert must "rebuild" a past mental state to help the judge assess guilty. The evaluator must understand the meaning of the relevant elements for the imputability of the mental state. The term *mens rea* be often used in assessments of criminal liability, but the term also assumes different meanings. More specifically and traditionally, the term *mens rea* refers to the specific mental state element that is necessary for committing a fact considered a crime. The mental state with which a crime is committed is a crucial criterion in which morality and criminal law identify an agent's fault in causing social damage because mental states point to an agent's attitude towards harm and rights / interests of citizens. However, theory that considers the action of the mental sufferer as a product of the disease itself, it can lead to assimilate erroneously not punishable action because of the infirmity to the concept of involuntary action. In fact, if it is stated that the subject is not responsible for the action, if it is determined that this is derived from infirmity itself, it appears that the subject is not punishable because the action should be attributed not to him but to the disease understood as "true "cause of action. Reasoning is somehow overturned, starting from the assertion that the judgment of infirmity must be based on the assessment of the retention of the general functioning of the mental mechanisms that the agent does, rather than the finding of a presumed "obscure force" which makes the actions of the free or involuntary subject. According to this theoretical point of view, people be characterized as being able to form the reasons for the act (cognitive aspect) and able to act concretely based on such reasons (strong-willed aspect). The theory of infirmity as irrationality evidently refers mainly to the cognitive aspect.

In the Italian penal system, the capacity of will is defined in the suitability of the subject itself to self-determine, in relation to the normal impulses that motivate the action, in a manner consistent with the values it carries, in the power to control the impulses to act and determine on the basis of the reason that seems more reasonable or preferable on the basis of a conception of value, in aptitude to handle an effective regulation of their own, free self-determination.

In Anglo-Saxon law, depending on the nature of the crime and the alleged cause of mental illness, there are three forms of defence that can be invoked; mental illness, less responsibility, and automatism. It is important to note from the outset that these definitions are legal and non-medical. Mental illness be relevant for imputability, the cause must it be attributed to "internal" factors to the individual; if the cause is exogenous then it be considered a case of automatism.

The strong-willed and cognitive aspect of mental illness relevant for forensic purposes has been formally united in the American Law Institute's Model Penal Code (MPC) of 1962. The MPC has in fact stated a person is not responsible for criminal conduct if at the time of such conduct as a result of mental disease or defect he lacks substantial capacity either to appreciate the criminality [wrongfulness] of his conduct or to conform his conduct to the requirements of the law. The psychic anomalies, in themselves, are not a cause of not imputability but must also lead to a further condition of inability to appreciate the injustice of their actions or to control their behavior. In England, the publication of the document Criminal Responsibility: Insanity and Automatism (Law Commission 2013) represents a significant attempt to develop appropriate premises for a revision of the law on mental disorders and criminal liability. The authors propose abolishing the defence of mental illness and a significant change in the concept of automatism, even in the light of other changes. In their place, the main reason for imputability will become "not criminally responsible due to a recognized medical condition". There are several points to point out with regard to the use of specific terms: firstly, the notion of "guilt" is replaced by "criminal liability" to adapt to the idea of ensuring that people be punish only for reasons which they are responsible for. Secondly, the emphasis on "recognized medical conditions" reflects the definition of infirmity resulting from the jurisprudential interpretation of "mental illness".

In the countries of juridical culture Anglo-Saxon the concept of "insanity", that is the correspondent of our "infirmity", is not a medical concept and for avail oneself of that "we must apply the law and not the medicine". Therefore, "the definition of the terms that appear in a law must be determined by the purposes of the law and not from conceptual categories borrowed from other disciplines". This principle has driven some philosophers of the right to argue that expert witness (psychiatrists) cannot and must not express themselves on the possible correlation between the medical conditions of the subject and responsibility for a particular action. They cannot because their scientific and professional competences would not provide them of valid judgement categories. Similarly, they should not be because this would represent a limitation of conceptual categories outside the law, and because the person would rely directly on the "experts" judgment and therefore, without having publicly recognized criteria, it would mean abandoning the concept of "fair trial".

However, this does not seem to be the current orientation in the Italian penal system, since judgment no. 9163 of Penal Court of Cassation United Sections of 2005 states that the judge cannot in any case renounce to the necessary cooperation between criminal justice and science, in the symbiosis of an empirical plan and a normative one. In addition, we can read "The judge can only refer to the scientific acquisitions that, on the one hand, are the most up-to-date, on the other hand, the most generally accepted, more shared ones, end up with generalization application practice of its scientific protocols".

In this perspective, the contribution of neuroscience could be to improve the "objectivity rate" and therefore also the scientific knowledge of the opinions of the experts, if it is true, as Stracciari, Bianchi and Sartori (2010) claim, methods of cognitive neuroscience could help this if we note that today it is possible to objectify the neural correlation of personality disorder. The serious personality disorder is more likely to have some of the microstructural correlations that can be highlighted at Voxel-based Morphometry (VBM), while mild personality disorder does not have these features. However, Merzagora (2011) notes that one might even wonder if until now the test obtained through the magnetic resonance would be able to satisfy the c.d. "Daubert Criteria" that American jurisprudence – but not only – requires to assess the testimony of the expert, i.e.: 1 Has the method been tested? 2 Has the method has been the subject of a large number of publications? 3 What is the percentage of error? To what extent has this method been accepted by Community science? According to Vul and Kanwisher (2010), research with Functional Magnetic Resonance Imaging (fMRI) tests would not be able to meet the error rate criterion. So Merzagora concludes that regarding the problem we're dealing with, it's like saying that cerebral imaging is not the today of probative assessment, but it may be his tomorrow.

Baird and Fugelsang (2004) identified Brain Imaging techniques as an opportunity to prove definitively the degree of maturity of a teenager, with the consequent legal effect of determining the impossibility to consider the defendant fully responsible for the criminal plan. All this is particularly important in a context such as the American one, in the past even the minors were condemned to the death penalty and only recently, the Federal Supreme Court ruled out this possibility, making explicit reference to the cerebral development of the teenager.

Analogous complexity be find in the evaluation, in medical and legal terms, of offenses committed by drug addicts. Dependence is linked to choices that are (potentially) advantageous in the short term, at the expense of long-term positive outcomes. However, association does not imply causality, and there are both evidence that impulsive traits can become more pronounced through the implementation of abuse behaviors and impulsivity is one of the risk factors for developing addiction. Increased impulsivity is the main example of brain changes that may occur with the development of addiction, others include changes in underlying habits, salience processing, self-consciousness and increased stress sensitivity, defined the dark side of addiction. Most neurobiologists recognize a pathogenetic model that includes all of the above-described changes (occurs at different stages of addiction), where initially there is increase of the reward and the saliency of the substances of abuse (positive reinforcement stage), followed by an automatic and habitual answer (compulsive phase); in the terminal phase replaced by anhedonia and use of the substance to counteract the adverse effects of previous use (negative reinforcement). If dependence were a brain disorder in which autonomous choice is compromised, it would be important to deliver this assertion in the debate on neuroscience and free will. Wegner (2004, p. 657) states in that regard:

> Most of us think we understand the basic issue of free will and determinism. The question seems to be whether all our actions are determined by mechanisms beyond our control, or whether at least some of them are determined by our free choice (...) However, it is important to distinguish between the actual mechanisms leading to action (which, as few will dispute, are produced by brain processes, given a learning history and genetic make-up), and the first-person feeling of free will.

According to Wegner, the will is a subject's own emotion, a somatic marker that distinguishes the author of the action as himself. This may or may not correspond to the real causes underlying the act but has a precise function: it allows us to maintain the sense of responsibility of our actions. In this sense, the disease has an effect on autonomy (or its counterpart, "free will") to lose itself in a state of dependence because the diseased brain determines the choices made in a reflex manner, based on precise environmental stimuli (related to addiction).

References

AA.VV. (1981) Lessico Universale Italiano. Istituto Italiano della Enciclopedia Italiana, Roma.
Austin J.L., (1961) *Philosophical Papers*. Clarendon, Oxford.
Baird A., Fugelsang J. (2004) "The emergence of consequential thought: evidence from neuroscience". In *Philos Trans R Soc Lond B Biol Sci*, 29; 359(1451), pp. 1797–804.
Deutschländer R., Pauen M., Haynes J.D. (2017) "Probing folk-psychology: Do

Libet-style experiments reflect folk intuitions about free action?" In *Consciousness and Cognition* 48, pp. 232–245.

Fenton T., Wiers R.W. (2017) "Free Will, Black Swans and Addiction". In *Neuroethics*, 10, pp. 157–165.

Frankfurt H. (1971) "Freedom of the Will and the concept of a person". In *The Journal of Philosophy*, LXVIII.

Hayakawa S., Costa A., Foucart A. and Keysar B. (2016) "Using a Foreign Language Changes Our Choices". In *Trends in Cognitive Sciences*, 20(11), pp. 791–793.

Glenn A.L., Raine A. (2008) "The neurobiology of psychopathy". In *Psychiatry Clin. North Am.*, 31(3), pp. 463–7.

Jaspers K. (1988) Psicopatologia generale (ed. italiana a cura di R. Priori). Il pensiero Scientifico editore, Milano.

Law Commission (2013) Criminal liability: Insanity and automatism. London, 23 July.

Libet B. (2009) *Mind Time: The Temporal Factor in Consciousness*. Harvard, Harvard University Press.

Libet B., Gleason C.A., Wright E.W., Pearl D.K. (1983) "Time of conscious intention to act in relation to onset of cerebral activity (readiness-potential). The unconscious initiation of a freely voluntary act". In *Brain*, 106 (Pt 3), pp. 623–42.

Libet B., Searle J. (2001) "Consciousness, free action and the brain". In *Journal of Consciousness Studies*, VIII.

Malle B.F. and Nelson S.E. (2003) "Judging Mens Rea: The Tension between Folk Concepts and Legal Concepts of Intentionality". In *Behavioral Sciences and the Law* 21, pp. 563–580.

Merzagora Betsos I. (2011) "Il colpevole è il cervello: imputabilità, neuroscienze, libero arbitrio: dalla teorizzazione alla realtà". In *Rivista Italiana di Medicina Legale*, vol. 1, pp. 175–208. Giuffrè, Milano.

Moore M.S. (1984) *Law and Psychiatry: Rethinking the Relationship*. Cambridge University Press, Cambridge.

Rhee S.H., Waldman I.D. (2002) "Genetic and environmental influences on antisocial behavior: a meta-analysis of twin and adoption studies". In *Psychological Bulletin*, 28(3), pp. 490–529.

Roskies A.L. (2010) "How does neuroscience affect our conception of volition?" In *Annu Rev Neurosci*.; 33, pp. 109–30.

Santoni De Sio F. (2013) *Per colpa di chi. Mente, responsabilità e diritto*. Raffaello Cortina Editore, Milano.

Stracciari A., Bianchi A., Sartori G. (2010) *Neuropsicologia forense*. Il Mulino, Bologna.

Vul E., Kanwisher N. (2010) Begging the question: the non-indipendence error in fMRI Data Analysis, Foundations and Philosophy for Neuroimaging. In Goodenough O.R., Tucker M. (eds) *Law and Cognitive Neuroscience, Annual review of Law and Social Science*, 6, pp. 61–92.

Wegner D.M. (2004). "Précis of the illusion of conscious will". In *Behavioral and Brain Sciences* 27: pp. 649–692.

Weygandt M., Wakonig K., Behrens J. et al. (2017) "Brain activity, regional gray matter loss, and decision-making in multiple sclerosis". In *Multiple Sclerosis Journal*, pp. 1–11.

Willmott C. (2016) Biological Determinism, *Free Will and Moral Responsability: Insight from Genetics and Neurosciences*. Springer.

4

The Importance of the Decision-making Factor in Canonical Marriage

CIRO PUNZO

The legal nature of marriage

Marriage derive etymologically from *mater e munus* (mother's duty). From this idea, I would think that it is necessary to move to understand how the indissoluble bond between intending spouses is the binding symbol of the love between Christ and the Church.

This union focuses not only on marriage *in fieri* (that is the constitutive moment of the marriage), but also *in facto* (in the conjugal relationship), as in both moments the decision-making factor that has 'created' (continuing on its mission) the life-long consortium is always present. The discipline of the general theory of canonical marriage law is essentially contained in the preliminary canons (1055–1062) of the current code of canonical law, which governs the marriage institution and its properties.

In order to enhance our topic in epigraph, I will begin with the canon 1055 until 1060. The canon 1055, about that, textually: "*1°. Matrimoniale foedus, quo vir et mulier inter se totius vitae consortium constituunt, indole sua naturali ad bonum coniugum atque ad prolis generationem et educationem ordinatum, a Christo Domino ad sacramenti dignitatem inter baptizatos evectum est. 2°. Quare inter baptizatos nequit matrimonialis contractus validus consistere, quin sit eo ipso sacramentum*". This norm provides a juridical description of the matrimonial institute, in which one finds the fundamental characteristic of marriage between baptized, perceived in its sacramental nature. However, the latter, which highlights the divine descent of marriage, does not fail, as widely recognized by the Church,

the nature of a natural institution, which is to be found in those peculi-
arities inherent in man and woman who, as sexed beings, are by nature
inclined to conjugal life. Therefore, the marriage-sacrament has a dual
nature: natural and divine. This conception assures a canonical over-
coming of the previous legal qualification, provided by the abrogated
Plan Code – Benedictine of 1917, which qualified marriage as a matter
of contractual nature and of interdependence, whose relative consensus
was based on it *ius in corpus* the right to the other's body, aimed at procreation. The actual setting, in fact, considers marriage an institution not
only of a contractual but sacramental nature, and above all personalist, as
the spouses freely make between them a pact, or tie, of a matrimonial
type. Consequently, the focus is on the *foedus*, which, without excluding
its contractual characteristic, appears, primarily, as an interpersonal relationship between the spouses. Thus, the centrality of the human nature
of marriage emerges, rooted in the will of intending spouses to form
consortium totius vitae. The latter belongs to a much higher legal rank, as
it simultaneously contains not only the realization of a life project
between two persons of different sex, but also the completion of one's
personal formation in the constitution with each other one flesh. I would
like to share the affirmation of a part of the doctrine, which considers
that, in the can. 1055

> it is outlined in its essential features that reality is Christian
> marriage as a community of people, a man and a woman, born of
> an irrevocable love affair by which spouses are given and received
> mutually in communication and giving to you the other of yourself.
> In addition, that conjugal pact, act of love that is the founding of
> marriage, is the fruit of freedom with which spouses decide to
> belong to themselves for the rest of their lives so as "not to be two
> but one flesh". So called to cooperate with the love of the Creator
> and the Saviour through them continually expanding and
> enriching his family. (Translation is mine, D'Auria 1997, p. 22)

Consequently, the consent of intending spouses presents a much
richer object than that contained in the previous canon code, moving on
the *consortium totius vitae*, in which the man and the woman – the two
people competing with the *foedus* – donate each other. From the aforementioned consortium, the following aims derive from which there is a
dense correlation: Hervada (2000) the love of spouses, the procreation
and education of the offspring. In fact, the *bonum coniugum* replaced *the
mutuum adiutorium et remedium concupiscence* of canon 1013 CIC '17,
rooted only on the mere physical act, but reduced to the "remedy" of lust.
Today the good of spouses is personified in love (even erotic and joyful

as they teach human sciences about sexuality in the state of marriage) and in mutual collaboration.

In order to verify the field of decision-making it is useful highlight, that the maturity of the individual subject is presupposed, which decides freely to form with its own part, even it aware, that unifying force that determines the aim mentioned. The unitive *vis* is perfected with openness to procreation, which should not be considered a mere physical act, or a continuation of the species, but as an act of collaboration with God's creative power, as well as the completion of the union of the two of a single flesh. It is clear that the nature of canonical marriage does not have only sacramental profiles, as the numerous studies on the juridical figure of marriage (Amenta 2013; Bertolini, 2008; D'Auria 2014; Diaz Dorronsoro 2014; Grocholewski 1978, 1996; Mingardi 2006; Ortiz 2010). Part of the doctrine believes that the marriage-sacrament has three deserving aspects of protection: the legal aspect (the contract), the sacramental aspect (a sensible and effective celebration of the invisible action of grace) and the perfecting element marriage, that is, the consummation or exchange of relation of one's own identity to the corporeal. Thus, in the sacrament, "the creational reality of the "conjugal pact" comes so it is assumed, in the supernatural order, as an effective sign of grace" (translation is mine. Navarrete 1993, p. 92); the same doctrine, analyzing the expression '*foedus*' (can. 1055 §1), contract (can. 1055 §2), consent of the parties (1057 §1), believes that such terminologies concern the same human act that becomes sacrament (Navarrete 1993). Following this stream, there are those who believe that the contract/sacramental binomial is inseparable, precisely because, thanks to baptism, there is the presence of a supernatural marriage (Berti 1992). During the revision of the Code-Plan Benedictine of 1917, the question of the separation between the contract and the sacrament came under a different angle. The Church questions about the behavior toward baptized persons, but not believers or not practicing, who intend to join in sacramental marriage; in particular, he wondered if it was more right to claim from them the faith and the adherence to the sacrament, or to prevent the canonical marriage . A first doctrinal thesis asserted that these intending spouses, though possibly unbelievers, having never lost the *ius connubii*, could become aware of the marriage decision, even if not sacramental, which they must, however, be recognized by the Church, although not celebrated in the faith. Another part of the doctrine, focusing on the intent to marry, claimed that the mere lack of faith does not necessarily coincide with the lack of will to celebrate a true marriage. Thus, if there was an intention to establish an exclusive and faithful bond with the other spouse, namely the establishment of the *consortium totius vitae*, be considered that there was still a will for marriage according to the design of God.

Even if the parties did not have full knowledge of them, or they were even atheists or unbelievers; it would be this right intention, which makes us assume that they intend to receive marriage as preached by the Church. If, on the other hand, the baptized, non-believing or non-practicing subjects expressly reject the ecclesiastical conception of marriage, with all its derivatives, then they could not absolutely be admitted to the conjugal celebration. Starting from the indivisibility of marriage, if two baptized decide to end their sacramentally sanctioned marriage and ask for a declaration of nullity, there are a number of issues related to the qualification of the spouse's free decision:

A. With the judgment of nullity, perhaps, you get an amnesty of the sacrament, *which does not belong to the pre-understanding of nonbelievers or atheists spouses*?

B. In the case of an affirmative answer to this first question, could the Ecclesiastical Tribunal ever sanctify a supernatural element, not dependent solely on the human decision of the spouses but by the autonomous dynamism of Divine Grace?

C. If the judge is a priest, his *decisum* fall within the responsibilities of the priesthood. Could is placed it in the same way as the assignment of a penance to a repentant and forgiven sinner?

D. If the judge is laic, how could he, being a humble mortal, sanctify a supernatural sacramental entity?

Contrary to this first hermeneutic address, there is the doctrinal current that he thinks there may be a separation between the contract and the sacrament, since in the sacrament one necessarily has to assume an act of personal faith in the sacramental value of marriage. In short, the existence of an established faith is the source of the same subjective possibility of receiving a sacrament (De Paoli 1988). I would imagine that the problem of nullity of marriage, embracing this second argument, would easily be resolved, as the judge (laic or presbyter) would only do the sanctioning of the marriage / contract and would thus pursue merely human action. With the judgment of nullity, the faithful might even make a possible new sacrament marriage, which would "replace" the former, thus saving his divine aspect, which characterized by his sacramental meaning.

Property of Marriage

The analysis of the institution of marriage and the weight of its decision-making apparatus for intending spouses would be incomplete without the examination of its essential properties (ie as such, ie independent of the decision of human subjects). The canon 1056 enact "*Essentiales matri-monii proprietas sunt unitas et indissolubitas, quae in matrimonio christiano ratione sacramenti peculiarem obtinent firmitatem*".

The rule in question governs the essential properties of marriage, which be found, in fact, in unity and indissolubility. The nature of marriage, as a personal and intimate community among spouses, claims the existence of such essential properties, which define the conjugal pact, giving it also a particular legal qualification. Before proceeding with the analytical description of the properties, it is necessary to open a bracket on the distinction, which I would think fundamental, between the essence (pact ontology), purpose and property (Bonnet 2002). The first concerns the ontology of a reality, its elements sufficient to identify it. The pith, being metaphysical, makes the covenant have its own origin and its own end that characterize it. Consequently, in order to attain its purpose, the essence be endowed with elements to attain it. At the same time, the property, which is not the entity, but identifies it by what is precisely that particular reality. In other words, the essence of marriage is the life-long consortium, so the properties that identify and integrate it are unity and indissolubility. I would consider it essential to emphasize that this concerns marriage in *facto*, while another background for the marriage is *fieri*. For the latter, the essence is the consensus, characterized by subjective ability (ability to understand and will, with relative decision) and objective (ability to fulfil marital obligations) of the intending spouses. It should be noted that the essential properties of unity and indissolubility must be related both to the conjugal consortium and to the matrimonial consensus, since if the essence of marriage is given by *consortium totius vitae*, to it must be added the essential properties, which identify it as such even without consuming the essence; from his song the marriage consent, the efficient cause of the *consortium*, he must necessarily compile those properties, for otherwise, the matrimonial essence, of which the properties already mentioned, may not emerge. Part of the doctrine emphasizes how these are

> Actually closely linked as two sides of the same medal. Indissolubility [...] is the fullness of unity, because the ability to be husband and wife unfolds in all its fullness and perfection only when it is orientated and unfolded in relation to a single woman or a single man, in such a way that death alone sets limits on that capacity. (Translation is mine, Moneta 1998, p. 31)

I would now look at the specific properties mentioned above. Unity indicates that conjugal union is realized between one man and one woman, so marriage is as monogamous and heterosexual. On the one hand, the doctrine believes that unity belongs to a concept derived from natural law (hence from the ontology of the matrimonial pact), on the other hand it places such essential property in a theological dimension, recognizing its origin in the divine will manifested by Christ in the Gospel, according to which the unity of constraint constitutes man and woman in one flesh (Vitali, Berlingò 2003). As regards the indissolubility, it expresses the concept of stability of the bond, in the sense that, once put into validity not be dissolved or ceased, except because of the death of one of the spouses. The *ratio* of indissolubility lies in the fact that mutual self-giving cannot be subject to time constraints, so that marriage is valid for the entire life of the spouses. Unity and indissolubility refer to every marriage, even to that of non-baptized ones. I would consider it very important to point out that it is from the latter (and not from the canon 1056 or from other Canonical norms of the CIC '83) that the concept of *bonum fidei* is drawn, which is the exclusion of fidelity in conjugal bond.

In Christian marriage, these essential properties acquire a particular and specific stability in virtue of the presence of the sacrament. In fact, the perpetual and exclusive marriage bond, which is established among spouses in every marriage (see canon 1134), assumes greater consistency in Christian marriage than non-sacramental marriage, where it can be annulled for the privilege of faith (see canons 1143–1147).

In conclusion, on the legal level, the properties of unity and indissolubility are safeguarded, for example, by means the image of the impediment of the bond (canon 1085), the assessment of the consensual capacity (canon 1095, 2° – 3°), with the requirement to exclude bigamy or divorce from the subject of the will, or with the nullity of the consensus by mistake that determines the will (canon 1099). For probation purposes, according to my modest thought, it would be enough to investigate three principles: a) the personality of intending spouse (in order to discover the existence or not of the adulterous tendency); b) the relationship between the different personalities of the intending spouses; c) the correspondence of marital rights and duties. In this regard, I would like to emphasize the subtle difference:

1. Anyone expressing, implicitly or expressly, temporarily or perpetually, the will to exclude their right to receive or to perform conjugal acts and grant their matrimonial consent, establishes the grounds for declaring nullity;
2. On the other hand, those who express their consent with the mere intention of not fulfilling the marriage obligations that in the end, at the request of the consort, comply.

The Matrimonial Consent

The canon 1057 has the following text "*1. Matrimonium facit partium consensus inter personas iure habiles legitime manifestatus, qui nulla humana potestate suppleri valet. 2. Consensus matrimonialis est actus voluntatis, quo vir et mulier foedere irrevocabili sese mutuo tradent et accipiunt ad constituendum matrimonium*".

The marriage agreement between spouses is based on a free act of conscious will, through which spouses decide and commit themselves to reciprocal and perpetual donation. The matrimonial consensus, which gives rise to the consortium of life among the spouses, represents the fulcrum around which the canonical discipline of the marital institution (Castaño 1990). Indeed, as stated in canon 1057, comma §1, consensus is the primary and essential source of marriage, which could not exist in its absence.

The act of consent is undoubtedly a voluntary act, a weighted decision, belonging to the inner and personal sphere of the subject, which needs to be extraneous in order to allow mutual knowledge of the intending spouses and to allow the person meeting the agreed wishes of the spouses (Gil 1985). The will, subject to the provision of consent, presupposes an earlier intention (a decision to marry) and a future will (concerning married foedus, which engages the spouses in a stable and indissoluble manner). While the former is always preceded by acts belonging to the intellectual sphere (like that of evaluation), as a result of which it becomes the subject of judgment of practical reason; the second is translated into a free act, the result of all the circumstances underlying the decision to be taken, which must be extraneous without any conditioning or coercion. The §1 of canon 1057 also identifies the concept of legal capacity of contractors, the legitimate manifestation of consent and its irreplaceability (Pellegrino 2002).

Legal abilities are a cornerstone of consensual freedom, in the sense that contractors must be exempt from the marriage impediments provided in canons 1083–1094. Concerning the legitimate manifestation of consensus, it should first be noted, that the act of will belongs to the internal subjective sphere: it follows that no one can be obliged to marry if he does not want him inside. Secondly, it must be emphasized that, given the contractual nature of marriage, belonging to the category of interpersonal relationships, the wishes of the two persons approaching the marriage must coincide, so it is necessary that the inside of each of them is clearly unambiguously externally. With regard to the irreplaceability of the consensus, governed by §1 of canon 1057, it must first be made clear that it refers to the absolute impossibility of any other factor – even human – to substitute the person of the contractor in the very personal, decisional and voluntary act, inherent in the choice of marriage. This assumption does not allow any derogation. For these reasons, consent is a key element of a valid marriage, so its absence or invalidity inevitably entails the invalidity of marriage. Consent, freely and validly granted by the spouses, confers on the conjugal relationship the character of intrinsic indissolubility, which implies the possibility of dissolution of marriage by the Church, if there is still no consummation; instead, afterwards, marriage acquires the character of extrinsic indissolubility and not be dissolved (D'Auria 2003). The §2 canon 1057 deals with the nature and object of the matrimonial consensus. Human decision-making be achieved through intellect and will, the first is to reach the knowledge of truth, the second to obtain as well as the intellect presents as true. In the case of marriage, which falls within the category of goods, consensus is certainly an act of will (acting in co-operation with the intellect), deliberate – since it requires an assessment (discernment or judgment) of the intellect about goodness marriage and knowledge of essential rights and duties – and free, as the consensual act must not be subject to external conditioning or coercion of any kind. The formal object of the matrimonial consensus is represented by the irrevocable foedus, understood as a pact freely and permanently sealed by the spouses.

> For the purpose of a valid marital consent, the concept of conjugal love is also relevant. Indeed, it is merely a marital love that makes possible the mutual recognition of spouses in the size of the consortium totius vitae, so marriage consent must necessarily translate into an act of love since, otherwise, it could not qualify as a consensus. According to De Luca: "Love, wanting the good of the other (amor benevolentiae tomistico) is an act of will and as such cannot and must not be more deceitful of relevance and judgment in law" (translation is mine. De Luca 1990, pp. 136). The matrimonial institution postulates the presence of a loving component, since only conjugal love can establish a stable and definitive bond, given the uniqueness of the person of the other consort. Married love represents the expression of the intentionality of doing well to the compartment in order to achieve that deep and indissoluble bond. Ultimately, the foedus matrimonialis, aimed at the constitution of the marriage bond, coincides with the act of love, through which the intending spouses proceed to reciprocal self-giving, unconditionally and totally; it follows that conjugal love is an integral part of the matrimonial consensus, which is the centre of gravity of each person's natural right to marry. In this respect, the ius connubii governed by canon 1058, which reads: "Omnes possunt matrimonium contrahere, qui iure non

prohibentur". It is the recognition of a right to every individual, that is, the right of every human subject to marriage, based on the natural disposition of the human being to constitute the conjugal bond. It qualifies as a natural and fundamental right of every individual, which not be affected by any limit, unless it is derived from the protection of a superior good (Moneta 2002). It can happen, though, under the can. 1077, §1, the Ordinary of the place may prohibit ius connubii both in the presence of a serious cause and in the time in which the same lawsuit, or in the case of a prohibition stemming from a judgment of nullity, or a decree of the same Ordinary. It should be noted that in case of non-application of the two mentioned vetita, will apply the canon 1059, which verbally states that: "Matrimonium catholicorum, etsi una tantum pars sit catholica, regitur iure non solum divino, sed etiam canonico, salva competentia civilis potestatis circa mere civiles eiusdem matrimonii effectus". The above-mentioned provision states the existence of the Church's competence with regard to marriage celebrated among Catholics; this competence originates from a theological dimension and in particular from the relationship between Christ and His Church, which leads to the latter being the only one capable of disciplining and judging the marriage between baptized, in virtue of the sacramental nature of marriage. In addition, there may also be cases in which the Church intervenes on the marriages of non-baptized, by virtue of the apostolic mission of bringing all the creatures of God closer to the salvific project realized in Christ. Therefore, it is precisely the sacramentality of constraint that is the essential requirement that rooted, through divine law, the competence of the Church. It should be clarified that the marriage of Catholics, if carried out under a concerted arrangement, are also subject to the authority of the civil authority, recognized by the Church, since marital reality is still a civic, as well as ecclesiastical reality. However, civil jurisdiction is held to respect for divine law and its competence is confined to the only civil effects of Catholic marriage. In other words, civil jurisdiction will only concern the economic regime, maintenance and the rest of the purely civilian aspects. Marriage favours the development of the favor iuris and in this regard, the canon 1060 provides "Matrimonium gaudet favore iuris; quare in dubio standum est pro valore matrimonii, donec contrarium probetur". This provision establishes a legal presumption of validity of the marriage relationship, unless there is evidence to the contrary. It guarantees the stability of the law and protects the legal principle of trust. In this regard, Dalla Torre observes:

The first part of canon 1060 can be understood as a summary formula of all the substantive discipline of marriage, directed to regulate the exercise of that *ius connubii* which is certainly a human right and forms the group of the rights own of the faithful (cf. can. 219). (Translation is mine, Dalla Torre 2002, p. 223)

The presumption in question will only be applicable if the marriage is at least as legal act and there is a need to rule on its legal compliance. The presumption of validity works especially with regard to marriages with civil effects already celebrated. The *ratio* of such tutelage lies in the protection of social, natural and religious values, which have been applied in the already initiated conjugal relationship. The latter triggers, on probative plane, a sort of reversal of the *onus probandi*, in the sense that the test will not be the validity of the marriage, which is presumed, but the nullity of marriage. This implies that the judge, in case of doubt, will have to rule on the validity of the marriage.

Conclusions

The marriage represents not only a religious dimension, but also a social and civil truth tied to the nature of the man and of the woman in indivisible manner. Many have been the various doctrinal influences that have allowed marriage to be the legal entity that is today. Among these, I would recall Saint Thomas Aquinas, who finds, in matrimonial reality, three fundamental criteria:

(a) The '*essentiam*'
(b) The '*causam*'
(c) The '*effectum*'

Voltaire defines marriage as a people's right. Marriage, in other words, is the conscious donation of offer himself to one's own partner, in order to form *one flesh*. This donation must be:

(1) Freedom: a liberating act, such as donation, must not be subject to any form of constriction.
(2) Total: From what has been said, one can say that the human being is completed offering himself to the neighbour, who can be God or his 'brother'. While the aforementioned donation does not require any improvement, the latter becomes a *condicio sine qua non* in the matrimonial institution. In other words, an act of copulation by 'new spouses' is required to ensure the birth of the

offspring. We must not forget what was said in the first Epistle to the Corinthians: "The wife is not the arbiter of her body, but she is her husband; likewise also the husband is not the arbiter of his body, but he is his wife" (1 Cor 7, 4).

(3) Exclusive: marital donation can only take place with respect to their own partner: "To the spouses, I order, not me, but the Lord: the wife does not separate herself by the husband and in case of the separation, to remain without getting married or to reconcile with her husband and her husband does not repudiate the wife (1 Cor 7, 10–11)".

(4) Definitive: The donation, to be called it such, must assume this characteristic; otherwise, there would be a loan.

(5) He must be heterosexual: "Do not you know that the unjust will not inherit the kingdom of God? Do not deceive yourself, neither the fornicators, nor the idolaters, nor the adulterers, nor the effeminate, nor the homosexuals" (1 Cor 6, 9–10).

(6) Must be fertile: Marriage, as mentioned above, involves the continuation of the species.

As noted, canonical marriage is highly protected by the manifestation of will expressed by two people approaching the marriage, who have become spouses. From it comes the implementation of the sacramental element of marriage, which is not identified as a property of the same, but as a transcendental aspect of the institute examined. In other words, the consent of the intending spouses not only results in the indissoluble bond between the same, but also the inseparable union of the same with God. Therefore, it is not necessary to be superficial in the pronunciation of the fateful 'yes', since not only is knowledge of the institute in question, in which ignorance is not admitted after the age of puberty but also full awareness of one's own *decisum*. The latter must not only be subjective, that is characterized by the maturity that qualifies the capable persons, but also objective, that is, the intending spouse must be predisposed and convinced to succeed in meeting the marital burdens. All this is of great importance as the basis, as we have been able to analyse, to realize a free personal introspection for the fulfilment of the *foedus* husband. The marriage decision is so significant that it is being investigated by the judges in matrimonial lawsuits, in which they scrutinize both the *excursus* of the spouses (family origins, reception of the sacraments, participation in the cult of the Church on the day of the Lord), and the behavior of the latter in the ante and post-matrimonial phases, in order to understand whether the consent was given in full conscience (D'Auria 2007).

56 | CIRO PUNZO

References

Amenta P. (2013) "Matrimonio tra battezzati e disciplina ecclesiale: quale il rilievo della fede personale dei nubendi?" In *Ephemerides Iuris Canonici* 53.

Gil F.R.A. (1985) *El nuevo derecho matrimonial canónico.* Universidad Pontificia de Salamanca: Biblioteca de la Caja de Ahorros y Monte de Piedad de Salamanca.

Berti M. (1992) *L'esclusione della sacramentalità del matrimonio da parte dei battezzati non-credenti nella dottrina e nella giurisprudenza attuali.* Dissertatio ad doctoratum, pro manuscipto, Trento.

Bertolini G. (2008) *Intenzione coniugale e sacramentalità del matrimonio.* Cedam, Padova.

Bonnet P.A. (2002) "Essenza, proprietà essenziali, fini e sacramentalità", *(cann. 1055–1056).* In AA.VVV., *Diritto matrimoniale canonico*, vol. I, Città del Vaticano.

Castaño J.F. (1990) "El canon 1057, centro de la legislacion matrimonial de la Iglesia". In *Revista Espanola de Derecho Canonico*, 47(129), pp. 563–575.

Dalla Torre G. (2002) *"Il favor iuris" di cui gode il matrimonio (can. 1060–1101, §1).* In AA.VV. *Diritto matrimoniale canonico*, vol. I, Città del Vaticano.

D'Auria A. (1997) *Il difetto di libertà interna nel consenso matrimoniale come motivo di incapacità per mancanza di discrezione di giudizio.* Lateran University Press, Roma.

D'Auria A. (2014) *Fede e sacramentalità del matrimonio. La prospettiva canonica.* In Diriat A., Salucci S.(eds.), *Fides – foedus. La fede e il sacramento del matrimonio.* Cantagalli, Siena, pp. 141–178.

D'Auria A. (2003) *Il matrimonio nel diritto della Chiesa.* Lateran University Press, Roma.

D'Auria A. (2007) *Il consenso matrimoniale Dottrina e giurisprudenza canonica.* Aracne, Roma, pp. 21–85.

De Luca L. (1990) "L'esclusione del "bonum coniugum". In AA.VV. *La simulazione del consenso matrimoniale canonico.* Città del Vaticano.

De Paoli G. (1988) "Fede e sacramento del matrimonio". In Zaggia C. (a cura di) *Matrimonio fede e sacramento, Tribunale Ecclesiastico Regione Triveneto.* Cedam, Padova.

Diaz Dorronsoro R. (2014) "Il carattere battesimale e il consenso matrimoniale". In Diriat A., Salucci S.(eds.), *Fides – foedus. La fede e il sacramento del matrimonio.* Cantagalli, Siena, pp. 123–139.

Hervada J. (2000) *Studi sull'essenza del matrimonio.* Giuffré, Milano.

Grocholewski Z. (1978) "Crisis doctrinae et iurisprudentiae rotalis circa exclusionem dignitatis sacramentalis in contractu matrimoniali". In *Periodica* 67, pp. 283–295.

Grocholewski Z. (1996) "L'esclusione della dignità sacramentale del matrimonio come capo autonomo di nullità matrimoniale". In *Monitor ecclesiasticus* 121, pp. 223–240.

Mingardi M. (2006) L'esclusione della sacramentalità del matrimonio. In *Quaderni di diritto ecclesiale 19*, 416–443.

Moneta P. (2002) "Il diritto al matrimonio (can. 1058)". In AA.VV. Diritto matrimoniale canonico, vol. I, Città del Vaticano, pp. 193–194.

Moneta P. (1998) *Il matrimonio nel nuovo diritto canonico*. Ecig, Genova.

Navarrete U. (1993). "Matrimonio, contratto e sacramento". In *Me* 118, 91–112.

Ortiz M.A. (2010) "L'esclusione della dignità sacramentale: la retta intenzione e
la disposizione per credere". In *Ius Ecclesiae 22*, 90–106.

Pellegrino P. (2002) *Il consenso e il suo oggetto (cann. 1057-1100-1107)*. In AA.VV.
Diritto matrimoniale canonico, vol. I, Città del Vaticano, p. 156.

Vitali E., Berlingò S. (2003) *Il matrimonio canonico*. Giuffré, Milano.

5

The Marriage Consent Invalidated by the Person's Error

Ciro Punzo

The problems of the Canon 1097, §1: "*Error in persona invalidum reddit matrimonium*"

What happens if the intending spouse convinced to contract an irrevocable *foedus* with a certain person, then finds out that, the latter has been "replaced" with another? In these cases, canon 1097 §1 intervenes, which declares the marriage null because the relative consent is spoiled by the factual error on the identity of the person, which, however, seems to be considered as physically present. Moreover, the current canon replaces that (can 1083, §1) of 1917, on which part of the doctrine he had asserted that personal error could only occur when the intending spouse wishes to celebrate the marriage "*cum persona certa ac determinata. E.g. Maria, filia Maevii, quae sit de facto persona absens et ignota; quod aliqua mulier praesens iactet se esse eam personam; quod ipse deceptus eam ducat in uxorem*" (Gasparri 1932, vol. II, 17–18, n. 790). In practice, this error seemed to be only applicable to marriage by proxy, or if there was a strong resemblance between the replaced person and the one actually present at the wedding. We wonder today whether the term person has only its own anthropological-biological value of meaning, or may imply anything else, as supported by the positive hermeneutic canon 96 of CIC '83, for which a person is constituted as such thanks to Baptism: *Baptismo homo Ecclesiae Christi incorporatur et in eadem constituitur persona, cum officis et iuribus quae christianis, attenta quidam eorum condicione, sunt propria, quatenus in ecclesiastica sunt comunione et nisi obstet lata legittime sanctio* (D'Auria 2001, p. 273; Thomas, pp. 1265–1274: "*quidam speciaiori et perfectiori modo invenitur particulare et individuum in substantiis rationalibus, quae habent dominium sui actus, et non solum aguntur, sicut alia, sed per se agunt [...] Et hoc nomen est persona. Et ideo in praedicta definitione personae ponitur substantia individua, in quantum significat singolare in genere substantiae: additur autem rationalis naturae, in quantum singolare in rationalibus substantiis*").

Pope Giovanni Paolo II, in the Allocation, held in the Tribunal of the Roman Rota on January 29, 1993, to safeguard an ancient hermeneutic criterion in personal configuration, stated that "it would be entirely arbitrary, but openly unlawful and severely censured to attribute the words used by the Legislator are not their 'proper' meaning, but those suggested by disciplines other than canonical. We cannot conceive in the interpretation of the current Code, a fracture with the past, as if in 1983 there had been a leap into a totally new reality in terms of error in person (can 1097 §1); the terms used by the Legislator are not allowed to attribute a meaning unrelated to the canonical tradition" (translation is mine). In fact, if the term 'person' means the code also meant 'personality' and therefore, if the hypothesis in which, for example, 'I wish to marry Maria Esposito as the same is generous' (would be, identifying the person Mary with her own personal qualities), she would have a conditional consensus, that is no longer centred on the physical identity of that person, but on the inner identity with some of her property (where the weight of the psychic aspects would be evident of the human person).

> However, if the concepts of person and personality were fungible, that is, whether the quality of such relief should be understood to substantially characterize the person, the identity of the person would disappear in the course of his existential relationship. In other words, the person remains the same even if a certain point in his life contracted a disease or commits an action (for example a serious offense) indelibly indicates his next life. Something that would not happen if the qualities defined the person in a "substantial" manner. (Translation is mine: Bianchi 1998, p. 43)

In spite of this decisive substantive orientation to be attributed to the term person, part of the doctrine has not failed to raise reservations about the term 'natural persons', noting that the human person is not only predominantly composed of the physical, somatic element (Navarrete 1998) , but his personal configuration should be extended to all those qualities that have a radical and decisive influence on the personality of it, both in terms of making it moral and existential in appearance to an individual substantially different from what appears to the outside at the time of performance of the matrimonial consent (Moneta 1994).

Therefore, the problem is condensed in the initial lines of this essay, or if the interpretation of can. 1097 §1 on the error of person, may be imposed only on the criterion of physical identity, or be understood according to a more comprehensive and complete vision of the human person (D'Auria 2001), which states that "in the new different canonical law it seems to have become the legal concept of person. This conclusion must now be considered peacefully acquired in the light of the new "personalized" conception of marriage highlighted by the Second Vatican Council and transposed by the Code. For 'person' today can no longer be understood only as being physical, but the individual as well as constituted by his physical, legal, moral and social qualities" (translation is mine: Gullo 1986). In this regard, part of the doctrine considers arbitrary the extension of the concept of person with aspects that pertain to the personality of the subject, as

> *con la excusa de la aplicaciòn de la norma personalista – segùn la cual, a entender de algunos, la persona no puede verse reducida a su mera individualidad fisica, sino que debe comprenderse en toda su riqueza y complejidad – se cometen abusos contra la persona, que se convierte en objeto de uso, precisamente lo que segùn la norma personalista se debe evitar.* (Franceschi 1996, p. 254)

Navarrete moves in the same direction when he states that

> [...] if in the whole CIC the concept 'person' has the [...] sense of [...] the subject of assigning the duties and rights of the Christian, in his individual identity, abstraction from any further quality [...] which foundation can be attributed a different meaning to the same term 'person' in c. 1097, since the legislature does not offer any element that could justify a different interpretation of the same noun". (Translation is mine: Navarrete 1998, p. 371)

For these reasons, it results no net at "*conatus laxandi compagem personae physicae in re matrimoniali sustineri nequit, si prae oculis habeatur principia interpretationis legum ecclesialium* (cf. can. 17)" (c. Stankiewicz, 1993, in Ius Ecclesiae, 6, 1994, 614, n.7), in order to draw the following conclusion: "*congruere omnino videtur cum doctrina canonica interpretata Codicem a. 1917, adeo ut alia significatio verbi 'personae' non inveniatur*" (c. Pompedda, 06. 02. 1992, in *Ius Ecclesiae*, 6, 1994, 582, n. 2/g).

It should be noted, however, that, looking at the jurisprudence of merit, does not follow the same hermeneutic path coram Canals (1970), which stated that psychological and moral qualities also identify the person.

However, this ruling was criticized by Pompedda, who considers that personal qualities, not be replaced by the person (c. Pompedda, 23.07.1980, in *SRRD*, 72, 1987, 524, n.5).

Comment on the Canon 1097 §2

Canon 1097 §2 *"Error in qualitate personae, etsi det causam contractui, matrimonium irritum non reddit, nisi haec qualitas directe et principaliter intendatur"*. The §2 clearly indicates the invalidity of marriage, only if there is a mistake about the direct and principal quality of the person in the compartment.

Canon 1083 §2 del CIC '17 he considered that the qualities of the person were only marginal to the validity of the consent of the intending spouse who contracted the marriage with a given physical part. As a result, there were at that time three doctrinal currents, which concerned the error of person:

1. The first concerned the error redundans, of which the Supplement to the Thematic Summit of Tommaso D'Aquino, which considered that there was no matrimonial nullity if the consent of the intended spouse relies on a particular person, on whom it also redefines the quality desired by the former. Different is the case where the consent be based on the certain personal quality, which is above the physical person of the partner. In this case, the marriage will be null (Thomas 1265–1274);

2. Sanchez believed that the quality error became a mistake about the quality of the person only when the latter was unknown to the intending spouse, which can only identify it with the said main quality (Sanchez 1863). Indeed, during the formulation of CIC '17.

   The ecclesial jurisprudence, and in particular the Roman [...] has been firm in its interpretation of the error on individual qualities. According to such a consistent case law 'error qualitatis in personam redundans respicere debet qualitatem plane individualem personae; error qualitatis in errorem personae dedundat, si quis volens contrahere cum quadam persona certa et per eam qualitatem determinatam, absente et ignota, deceptus ducit mulierem hanc praesentem, quae sese fingit illam personam esse; non enim differt, sive personam determinans nomine sive qualitate individuali'. The ecclesial jurisprudence, and in particular the Roman, was therefore strictly adherent – and in fact remained univocal until 1970 – in his interpretation of the personal mistake of individual qualities to the traditional setting [...] thus contributing ... to consolidating an important canonical tradition whose roots emerged at least [...] at the time of [...] Thomas Aquinas". (Translation is mine: Bonnet 1987, pp. 99–100)

3. St. Alfonso M. de Liguori outlined three rules:

(a) The first is that the redundant error becomes the main reason for the consensus of the intending spouse, in such a way as to render marriage void.
(b) The second is based on the identity between the qualitative errors, which becomes a mistake on the person
(c) The third is because redundant error is based on the person already known by the intending partner.

In other words, if I say 'I want to marry Tizia, whom I consider high-ranking', marriage is not null, because there is the will to marry 'Tizia', which is not 'overwhelmed' by its quality of 'being high-ranking'. Following the third rule of St. Alfonso, we came to the current §2, which concerns a consensus based solely on a certain quality, so that the holder of the latter is irrelevant. In other words, it is as if I said 'I want to marry a lawyer'. Consequently, this quality must exist before the consensus is formed and must be the only determined object on which is based the certainty of access of marriage. Therefore, continuing the example does not matter that this quality is Caio or Tito, the important thing is that its possessor has one of these quality features. From this point of view, we can deduce that this precise will of the intended spouse not be replaced by an interpretative will, that is from a "supposition of modification of the proposed marriage ... and must not be confused with that was his consent to the moment he contracted (the colloquial expression and frequent 'I would not been married now if I had knew' then what she was supposed to want now, but not was what then she really wanted" (translation is mine: Viladrich 2001, p. 205). Ultimately, lacking at the time of consensus, this direct quality "falls into an element that was not only decisive in the marriage decision but had a close orientation towards choosing a certain person, leaving it in second plan any other dowry or personal connotation showed" (translation is mine: Moneta 1995, p. 150).

Conclusions

Canon 1097, §1 is, as we have seen, on the error of the person that the intending spouse may encounter, if you consider absent-mindedly the part that, in reality, is physically absent and is likely to resemble a person on the altar present. §1, therefore, is based on the physical identity of the person who, according to my modest opinion, cannot be replaced by qualitative identity and cannot be included in the complexity of the term person because, if so, the §2 of the same canon would exist. Indeed, the latter, based on the determining and main quality of a partner, not only causes marriage nullity (since the consent is rooted not on the 'owner' of the same quality, but exclusively on the latter), but I would think that it can be 'labelled' as a 'subjective element', which differs from the objective one represented in the physical body of the partner. I would therefore consider that the relevant evidence, in the case of a nullity judgment, is represented in the understanding of the error, in the direct evidence (including the confession of the person who falls into error) and indirect evidence, concomitant and subsequent to the marriage) for which, after learning of being mistaken, a strong reaction from the intending spouse (D'Auria 2007).

References

Bianchi P. (1998) *Quando il matrimonio é nullo? Guida ai motivi di nullità matrimoniale per pastori, consulenti e fedeli.* Giuffré, Milano.

Bonnet P.A., (1987) "Creatività giurisprudenziale ed errore personale sulle qualità individuali (un tentativo di più adeguata comprensione e tutela del sentimento religioso matrimoniale nel diritto ecclesiale)". In *Il Diritto Ecclesiastico*, 98, I, pp. 99–100.

D'Auria A. (2001) "Errore e consenso matrimoniale: rilievi interpretativi". In *Apollinaris*, 74 (1–4), pp. 257–275.

D'Auria A. (2007) *Il consenso matrimoniale Dottrina e giurisprudenza canonica.* Aracne, Roma, pp. 277–323.

Franceschi H. (1996) "Algunas consideraciones sobre el error de hecho – en la persona o en sus cualidades – y su la relaciòn con el error dolosamente causado". In AA.VV. *Curso de derecho matrimonial y procesal canònico para profeionales del foro*, vol. XII, Salamanca, p. 254.

Gasparri P. (1932) *Tractatus canonicus de matrimonio*, Città del Vaticano, vol. II, 17–18, n. 790.

Gullo C. (1986) *Note minime su retroattività e rapporto fra par. I e II del can. 1097, CIC.* In *Il Diritto Ecclesiastico*, 97, II, pp. 363–364.

Moneta P. (1995) *Il matrimonio nel nuovo diritto canonico.* Ecig, Genova.

Navarrete U. (1998) "Error in persona (c. 1097 §1)". In *Periodica*, 87, pp. 363–371.

Sanchez T. (1863) "De sancto matrimonii sacramento". In *Liber VII*, disp. XVIII, n. 38, Venezia, p. 69.

Thomas S. *Summa Theologie, Supplementum.* Pars III, q. 51, art.2, 1265–1274.

Thomas S. *Summa Theologiae.* Pars I, q. 29, art.1, 1265–1274.

Viladrich P.J. (2001) *Il consenso matrimoniale. Tecniche di qualificazione e di esegesi delle cause canoniche di nullità (cc. 1095–1107 CIC).* Giuffré, Milano.

6

The Role Exercised by Ignorance in the Matrimonial Institute: Social and Educational Profiles in the Performance of Consensus

CIRO PUNZO

Canon 1096 §1: Reflections on the *ignorantia*

Canon 1096 CIC 1983 recites: "*1° Ut consensus matrimonialis haberi possit, necesse est ut contrahentes saltem non ignorent matrimonium esse consortium permanens inter virum et mulierem ordinatum ad prolem, cooperatione aliqua sexuali, procreandum. 2° Haec ignorantia post pubertatem non praesumitur*". Unlike the intellectually and voluntarily incapacitating of the intending spouse or the relative inability to fulfil the rights and duties deriving from the conjugal relationship, the hypothesis of *ignoratia* transforms the *iter* of the formation of consensus.

This is because the focus is no longer on the analysis of psychological disorders or personality disorders related to the voluntary and intellect sphere of intending spouse, but to external phenomena such as the socio-cultural environment and the family and educational context in which the contractor has grown up and developed, which may well have had an impact on knowledge *in re matrimoniali*, also conditioning the matrimonial consensus to be given.

Ignorance also relies on the psycho-relational part of the subject, therefore diminish or deprive of all, the integrity of the intellectual psychic process that must characterize the act of consent, also influencing the strong-willed process, since it is possible to want only within the limits of all that known. According to classical doctrine, the error lies in a *falsa rei apprehensio*; ignorance is a *carentia debitae scientiae*, that is a defect of science that should be supposed to exist; the ignorance concerns the subject who, due to lack of information received from the educational and socio-cultural context, ignores that the other person, due to his personal condition, is still unable to know; the inadvertence concerns the lack of practical knowledge regarding the free act.

Marriage Consent is a human act necessary for the intending spouses to wish the conjugal object. Of course, they will need to have specific knowledge, since no one is able to give consent if he ignores the object to which his own psychic and relational act is directed. For this reason, it is necessary to conclude the intellect in the voluntary-consensual act, in order to give the will to that knowledge of the nature of the marriage relationship, without which it could not give rise to the decision-making process regarding the celebration of the marriage it would lack the indispensable perception of its object. You want to refer to a *minimum knowledge* that intending spouses have to have to give a valid consent, limited to the essential contents of marriage. Canon 1096, §1, which implements the general rule of canon 126 on the invalidity of legal acts, properly concerns matrimonial consent where it states that for its subsistence it is necessary that spouses do not ignore that marriage is the permanent community of men and women, ordained to procreate the offspring through sexual co-operation. This canon almost completely reproduces the lexical formulation of canon 1082, §1 CIC 1917 and could not be otherwise, because in those which are the essential elements for everyone about the nature or identity of marriage, *non datur variatio* (Parisella 1988). In this respect, you think the can.1096 constitutes a postulate derived from the same natural right (Pompedda 1993). Marriage is a natural as well as a juridical institution and, in the sacrament a supernatural institution: "Being deeply inserted into the original order of human society, there is a natural inclination towards it that leads every man to grasp it intuitively and spontaneous the essential and characterizing core" (translation is mine. Moneta 1998, p. 111). The natural inclination of man to marriage is explicated, from the codifying normative value to the can.1058: 'Omnes possunt matrimonium contrahere, qui iure non prohibentur' (Vitali, Berlingò 2003, p. 69). The now abrogated Benedictine code already outlined the features of canonical marriage through canon 1082 CIC 1917, which governed the minimum essential requirements of the *societas matrimonialis* that every intending spouse was obliged to know, even to a minimum, and the canon 1081, which defined marriage consent as an act of will aimed at the exchange between the contractors of the *jus in corpus perpetuum et exclusivum*. Canon 1096 of the current canon code has not brought any substantial changes to the discipline contained in the previous regulatory code setting. In addition, it should be noted that the Benedictine code-plan of 1917 used the expression "*cooperatione aliqua corporali*", creating a doctrine and jurisprudence dispute over the minimum level of knowledge of the physiological dynamics of the sexual sphere, necessary in matrimonial terms for the validity of conjugal. The *quaestio iuris* consisted in determining whether the necessary *scientia minima* should include the knowledge of the intending spouses about sexual sphere be realized in marriage; the debate is on both the doctrine and the jurisprudence, where there is a lack of the guidelines expressed in this area by the Tribunal of the Roman Rota. According to a first thesis called "minimalist", for the validity of marriage it was not necessary to have the full meaning of the sexual dimension, or else : "*coniugalis copulae, ne vagam quidem seu confusam*" (Grazioli, 20.1.1926, in *SRRD*, 18 (1935), 4; c. Jullien, 17.3.1926, in *SRRD*, 18 (1935), 68; c. Di Felice, 13.11.1956, in *SRRD*, 48 (1965), 892–893, n. 3; cfr., anche Lorenc 1953, 366–367), according to Sanchez's statement, for which: "*consensus efficiens matrimonium non fertur esplicite in copulam, sed in potestatem, et implicite in copulam*" (Sanchez Liber II, disp. 28, 1863). According to other doctrinal and jurisprudential principles called "maximalist", the spouses had to have a clear knowledge of the sexual dimension and not just the spiritual one of the marriage, for which:

"no precise idea of marital relationships is required, but at least the obligation of the concubine has to be fulfilled, and that it is to be understood that jus in corpus presupposes a material approach by acts which are exclusive to sexual life they are of no other relationship". (Translation is mine: Jemolo 1942, p. 239)

Intermediate positions include the thought of those (Lefebvre, 08/07 1972, SRRD, 64, 1981, 423, n.3) claiming that the reciprocal *deditio* of *jus in corpus*, as for canon 1081 CIC 1917 , he presumed that the couple should be aware of the need for co-operation for the generation of the offspring, but that this cognition was not specified in detail. A turning point in such a legal debate is found in the *decisio coram* Sabattani of 22 March 1963 in which the *Ponente* marries the "maximalist" orientation, asserting that, for the proper wedding celebration, the intending spouses must know the necessity of a "*mutuus concursus physicus ponendus per quaedam organa specifica, huic operi aptata et propria*".

It follows that any relevance *contra validitatem* may have the ignorance or error that falls on the modalities of sexual intercourse (Sabattani, 22.02.1963, in SRRD, 55, 1972, 207, n.13). The scope of the debate was greatly reduced by the issuance of canon law 1096 of the new Code of 1983 and, in particular, by the use of the expression "*cooperatione aliqua sexuali*". Indeed, the conjugal relationship that is created through the reciprocal tradition and *acceptatio suipsius* (canon 1057, §2) presupposes the spiritual, physical and sexual union of spouses so that, for the purposes of marriage, it is sufficient that the compartments do not ignore the characteristic of the conjugal relationship, understood as a state of permanent communion of life, predisposed to the procreation of the offspring through sexual cooperation, for their mutual completion. I would argue that with the expression "do not ignore" it is meant to refer to a common, popular and natural knowledge, not pretending to be a precise or scientific cognition. I would consider that the minimum knowledge required by canon 1096 should contain the following contents: a) *consortium permanente*, which indicates stable union and sharing among spouses. In other words, for the purpose of applying the aforesaid canon, there must be only the knowledge that conjugal status presupposes a permanent commitment, other than a transitional relationship; b) *between a man and a* woman belongs to a requirement of a natural nature that concerns the heterosexual nature of the marriage union, since the *consortium* is only possible between people of different sex as ordered specifically for procreation; c) the latter is achieved through sexual co-operation: this term refers to the fact that it is sufficient for intending spouses to be aware of the need for collaboration between their body and their genital organs.

Comment on §2 of the Canon 1096 and Probes

Moving now to the examination of n. 2 of the canon 1096, one can easily detect the existence of a *praesumptio iuris* for which the minimum knowledge inherent in the conjugal relationship acquires after puberty and, specifically, after 12 years for the woman and after 14 for the man, for which only before such age limits supposes ignorance in *re matrimoniali*.

The *ratio* of presumption contemplated by the code is to be found in the nature of such a minimum knowledge that each must possess, *naturaliter*, when, by puberty, it becomes capable of procreating. This type of presumption admits opposing when the framework educational, cultural, religious, family or environmental has hindered the formation of such knowledge in the subject. In that case, ignorance will have to be rigorous object of test, whether it is to prevent marriage in the puberty, or if the action of nullity is directed towards a marriage celebrated after puberty. Canon 1096 currently has little practical application. That said, it is interesting to specify the test criteria of this chapter of nullity of marriage. The first is surely the investigation of the biographical life of the subject and, therefore, of the analysis of the educational and training context of the intending spouse, as well as a review of environmental, family and socio-cultural factors that have influenced its development and its process of maturity in terms of what is also implicated in the sex sphere of intending spouses. These elements, confirmed by the statements made by the parties and witnesses, may have caused a complete ignorance of the characteristics of the matrimonial institute (Lefebvre, 8.7.1972, in *SRRD*, 64 (1981), 425, n. 9: "*Itaque partium declarationes maximi sunt momenti sive de mentis forma assertae ignorantis, sive de prima saltem reactione qua ostentus est cognitionis defectus*"). The before marriage relationship may already be a sign of lack of knowledge in *re matrimoniali* situations where symptoms of poor implementation of a parity relationship emerge. Similarly, other probative clues can be represented by cd. the criterion of post-marriage test, that is to say, from the actual arrangements for the conjugal consortium at the time of marriage, such objective historical facts will prove to be decisive in favour of probative arguments *pro nullitate* o *pro validitate*. It must be pointed out, however, that probationary proof of probability of nullity of marriage for ignorance under ex-canon 1096 is difficult to prove, since in most cases the minimum knowledge required by the contractors is owned by each individual by virtue of a natural process; it is also necessary to overcome the legal presumption set out in n. 2 of the canon in question. Ultimately, I would like to see that, in order to achieve a fully-fledged consensus, two conditions must be met a) a minimum knowledge of the partner; b) a minimum level of preparation for the marriage institute, as a specific legal entity. Only in this way is the realization of the conjugal foedus, which will not fall prey to such marital impediments as, in addition to the epigraph of the subject, the fraud and the error of law that I will analyse in subsequent contributions.

Decisions *pro e contra nullitatem*

The case law of the Roman Rota, even if it is dated, acknowledges that the head of nullity in question arises in situations of extreme and obvious ignorance expressed by the spouse, resulting from having lived in a particular environmental, educational and family context. Indicative in this regard is the case examined by the Corfe Lefebvre on July 8, 1972 (in SSRD, 64, 1981, 426, no. 13), in which the woman was convoluted to wedding without knowing how the children were born. She, indeed, before and after the wedding celebration, realized she did not have the slightest idea of what was sexual intercourse between spouses; it seemed inert and did not participate either psychologically or physiologically in the act of intimacy. The reason for such ignorance has been attributed to a too close and severe education given by the family, which has caused an aversion to the conjugal coexistence with the spouse, experienced in a traumatic way. Another case examined in the *decisio coram* Teodori of 24 June 1945 has a connection between ignorance and consensual inability: from a discussion of the fact, it is argued that the head of nullity of ignorance is absorbed by that of the consensual inability, resulting almost consequently and thus losing its legal autonomy. In Masala's *Coram* of 30.3.1997 (SRRD, 69, 1987, 168, 11), there is a clear case of ignorance stemming from a strict family education: the intending spouse, in fact, claims to be convinced that the children would be born simply being embraced. The *Coram* of Teodori of 8.7.1949 deals with ignorance of the intending spouse in relation both to the necessity that the conjugal relationship is necessarily heterosexual and to the need for sexual conjunction for the purposes of procreation of the offspring. From the spouse's testimony, it emerges that the woman had been very happy that her husband was a doctor, asserting that she could have taught her how to do the children because, in her opinion, when she asked for explanations mother and aunt, the latter had replied that they did not remember it. From this, she was convinced that she needed injections to have a child. However, the woman in question has actually shown reluctance towards the conjugal copula and this is a probative indication of the existence of ignorance, especially where the hostility towards sexual intercourse persists after the first attempt to consume. As of the *decisiones pro validitate*:

(1) c. Parrillo, 20. 07. 1929 (in *SRRD*, 21, 1937, 310, nn. 6–7):

> I knew that marriage meant to be together, and when I was a girl I had seen that my father and my mother were together in the same bedroom and slept in the same room [...] I always thought before marriage that I would have children, but without knowing how to produce it [...] So, I then waited to be able to become a mother [...] but I did not know how such things would have happened [...] I only knew this, that after the marriage children were born: I truly believed that it was impossible to have children before marrying. I knew the baby came out of her mother's body, but all the fact for me was a mystery [...] Ex his quisque concludet Luciam non ignorasse, quae iut ut minimum exigit ad matrimonialem consensum habendum, nempe matrimonium esse societatem permanentem cum viro ad filios procreandos. Utique ignorabat, si ei stemus, modum usus coniugalis, et pressius per quaenam organa matrimonio utendum sit [...] Sed hoc non pertinet nisi ad scientiam usus matrimoniii, quam dicunt scientiam physiologice exactam copulae carnalis. (Translation is mine)

(2) c. Mannucci, 30. 07. 1927 (in *SRRD*, 19, 1936, pp. 353–354, n.5):

Were you without cognition about sex trade, coexistence, gener-
ating children? Answer: 'I knew that spouses did not live as
brothers and sisters. I knew that marriage was a lasting union
between man and woman'. Pressius questioned 'Did you possibly
think that man and woman lived together without any sexual
intercourse? Answer: 'I had an unclear idea of corporal and sexual
approaches. That the spouses sleep together, also the children
know it, though not pondering why [...] 'Before to marrying, I
knew that the children are produced in marriage by bodily touch
between man and woman, and that the children are then produced by the father and the mother together'. *Et pressius limitat
quae ignoraverit, nempe determinatum modum generationis*: 'I did
not exactly know what happening between man and woman to
produce their children' [...] 'I had been told several times by my
boyfriend and by confessor, but I did not want to know and I did
not think about it. I knew (*quod mihi satis erat*) the essentials.'
(Translation is mine)

These decisions of Roman Rota, on the other hand, have adversely
affected the declaration of nullity of marriage for the head of ignorance.
Such negative pronouncements are characterized by an equally rigorous
argumentative and evaluative approach that examines the problem of
defining the content of *jus in corpus* in its actual operational dimension,
aimed at procreation. The jurisprudence of the Roman Rota, in the
silence of canon 1082, §1 CIC 1917 (now filled with the expression "*cooperatione aliqua sexuali*" under canon 1096, §1 CIC '83), had to define the
concept of knowledge of the act sexual intercourse by spouses. According
to the widespread opinion, it was sufficient, for the sake of the invalidity
of consensus, to have a vague knowledge of the unifying phenomenon
and the *commixtio corporum*. Therefore, it was not possible to give to ignorance the reason of double maternity if the spouse, even though he does
not know how the offspring is born, proves to have basic elementary
knowledge of the matrimonial state of life. Indeed, in this case, according
to the jurisprudence of merit of that time, the contractor knows that
specific *minimum* and based on the marital status and its essential
purpose. Consequently, a vague knowledge of this can serve as a disabling
requirement for the maternal consensus on ignorance (D'Auria 2007).

References

D'Auria A. (2007) *Il consenso matrimoniale Dottrina e giurisprudenza canonica*.
Aracne, Roma, pp. 259–277.

Jemolo A.C. (1942) *Il matrimonio nel diritto canonico*. Giuffré, Milano.

Lorenc F. (1953) "De ignorantiae influxu in matrimoniali consensu". In *Apollinaris*, 26, pp. 366–367.

Moneta P. (1998) *Il matrimonio nel nuovo diritto canonico*. Ecig, Genova.

Parisella I. (1988) "L'ignoranza in re matrimoniali". In AA.VV. *Il consenso matrimoniale. Dallo jus conditum allo jus condendum*, Studia et documenta Iuris Canonici moderante Pio Fedele, Roma.

Pompedda M. F. (1993) "Annotazioni sul diritto matrimoniale nel nuovo codice canonico". In Pompedda M.F. *Studi di diritto matrimoniale canonico*. Giuffré, Milano, p. 208.

Sanchez T. (1863) *De Sancto matrimonio sacramento*, Liber II, disp. 28, Venezia.

Vitali E., Berlingò S. (2003) *Il matrimonio canonico*. Giuffré, Milano.

7

The Figure of the Fraud in the Matrimonial Consensus

PUNZO CIRO

The Canonical Notion of Fraud: Critical Analysis

The canon 1098 CIC 1983 expressly states "*Qui matrimonium init deceptus fraud, ad obtinendum consensum patrato, circa aliquam alterius partis quali-tatem, quae suapte natura consortium vitae coniugalis graviter perturbare potest, invalide contrahit*".

The legal case of the fraud, as a disabling element of the consensus, is an absolute novelty in the systematic codification of the actual matrimonial nullity, but with not a few psycho-relational implications.

It is therefore necessary to refer to some general features of the fraudulent figure in the legal act, since the canon 1098 is a specification of the general rule contained in canon 125 and affects a substantial element of the matrimonial institution (Garcia Martin 1999). The canon 125 expressly states "*§1 actus positus ex vi ab estrinseco personae illata, cui ipsa nequaquam resistere potuit, pro infecto habetur. §2 Actus positus ex metu gravi, iniuste incusso, aut ex fraud, valet nisi aliud iure caveatur; sed potest per senten-tiam iudicis rescindi, sive ad instantiam partis laesae eiusve in iure successo rum sive ex officio*". The second paragraph of the abovementioned provision examines the link between the fraud and the legal act, by deciding the validity of the latter by the first on the basis of the allegation that the voluntariness of *deceptus* is only faint, but not canceled, since the he does not annihilate the consensus which, however, is spoiled, even if not in such a way as to completely undermine the will expressed. The Legislator therefore makes an exception in view of the existence of legal acts which, on the other hand, require full freedom and voluntariness (hence the parenthesis "*nisi aliud caveatur*"); there is also the possibility of termination of the act by judgment of the court, either by office or by party request. The rescission action is relative, in the sense that it is that can be taken to court only by the subject for protection of which it is by law laid down; Moreover, it has constitutive nature as it has the effect of modifying or extinguishing an existing legal situation.

In order to be able to act the *actio rescissoria*, the act must have been put into effect *ex fraud* or under the direct influence of the fraud, so that the connection between the accomplished act and the perpetrated artifice is evident; it is also necessary to demonstrate the existence of the fraud in order to recognize the limitation of freedom suffered by the *deceptus* inasmuch:

> "the legislator deems invalidated some acts of major importance, both because of the common good of the Church and for the good of the people directly concerned (...) the exceptions *ex lege* to the general rule that sanctioned the validity of the act concerned mainly deal with cases of fraud "*circa accidentalia*" and sanction the invalidity of the act as the result of a decisive intervention of the ecclesiastical legislator". (Translation is mine. Palombi 2001, p. 68)

The positive set of rules provides, in such a way, guarantee and tutelage the consensual freedom, by means of the rescinding action instance of the *nubentes* (ex can. 1098). In the conjugal relationship, indeed, the fraud rises to the vice of consensus, from which the positive norm tends to protect the intending spouses, in order to safeguard their freedom of choice. The canon 1098 examines the misconduct caused by the conduct of one of the spouses or a third party affecting the quality of one of the contractors at the expense of the other and which may be prejudicial to the future conjugal life. The *ratio* that led to the establishment of the figure of the fraud lies in the will of the Legislator to protect the consent and freedom of the intending spouses, in order to ensure that determination to the matrimonial contract is genuine, conscious and autonomous. In fact, the deception inherent in the fraud draws on the very decision-making moment that the spouse's choice is made by the intending spouse. The discipline tends to safeguard the good faith of the latter and the freedom of his consensus, rather than sanction the wrongful act committed by the cheat. If we want to give legal co-ordination to the fraud, it should be pointed out that at least two subjects are involved in this legal case: the *deceptor* who does the fraud and the *deceptus* who undergo it; It follows that, for the first subject, the fraud acts as an act of will, in the second as act acting on the intellect and, consequently, on the will. In practice, fraud does not directly cause consent to a legal act, but a mistake in the intellect of the victim, who erroneously performs an act of will because of the false intellectual qualification of the act. In other words, the fraud immediately affects the intellect and across media way the will, so that the voluntary act with which a legal act is made is directly influenced by the error and only indirectly by the fraud.

This legal form is therefore classifiable in the category of vices of consensus *ex parte intellectus*, not *ex parte voluntatis*: in fact, the will of the contractor exists, however, it is generated on the basis of false information and then transmitted from the intellect, so it will be spoiled as directed towards a false reality (according to the thomist principle that the will chooses as the intellect has presented them as well to do). The effects produced by the fraud are the mistake and the ignorance, that why sometimes it is also defined as a fraudulent mistake. It should be added that the fraud presupposes, by the *deceptor*, the intent of deceiving, thus misleading the freedom of the *deceptus* that under normal conditions would lead to a different decision.

Until now, the one examined here is the so-called *dolus determinas or dolus causam dans*, also known as antecedent fraud (contrasted with *dolus incidens*). The latter motivates the *deceptus* to put in place the legal act and thus places itself as a causal link, albeit indirect, between the deliberate deception and the realized act.

The Code of Canon Law of 1917 did not contemplate the figure of the fraud as the cause of the invalidity of the matrimonial consent, since the Legislator had placed this case in the institution of the error referred to in the canon 1083 CIC 1917. The neutrality of the figure of the fraud was derived from the medieval type theory of *dolus in spiritualibus* (Fedele 1941; 1964), according to which, can be no cheated a subject who has benefited from the supernatural grace resulting from the sacrament. Such a theory has the limit of not considering the fraudulent effects, that is, error or ignorance, which distort the will of the subject. In the *tridentine* and *post-tridentine* period, this argument was overcome in favour of the recognition of the aberrant scope of the fraud as a defect of consensus: however, the error caused by the fraud had to be the subject of substantial error in order to take invalidation (Gasparri 1932). In this perspective, the quality error was of no relevance, as, by affecting accidental elements, it would not have a detrimental effect on the will, though always oriented towards the *substantia matrimonii*. From these arguments came the discipline of the factual error, contained in the CIC '17 at the canon 1083. Subsequently, it was the case-law of the Roman Rota to bring the fraudulent case into one of the three cases referred to in the aforementioned provision of the current Code, qualifying it as an indirect cause of error defying the consent, in the event that the error was the subject of an essential element of marriage, or what a vice of will. The canonical doctrine (Ferrata 1972) after the Code of 1917 debated the need to confer autonomous juridical relevance, in an invalid way, in the case of the fraud.

At the end of a long doctrinal debate on the interpretation of the cause of double maternity, or as a neutral case, the current canon 1098 of Code the 1983, which places the institute of the fraud in the category of matrimonial nullity; however, there no lack interpretative questions about the actual scope of the institute. In the period preceding the issuance of Code of 1983, there were doctrinal theses aimed at framing the fraudulent case in the category of impediments, in order to avoid the fracture of the marital shop due to a misleading conduct affecting moral or physical qualities, able to distort the will of the intending spouse (Mantovani 1972). The question of the development of a canon concerning the *impedimentum deceptionis* was dealt with by the doctrine of the early sixties, assuming two different directions: on the one hand, to create a general and abstract rule that governed just the case of error on a objectively a grave quality; On the other hand, it was for a discipline that enacted in a peremptory way a *numerus clausus* of pre-determined grave quality , which, if produced by the fraudulent error, involved matrimonial invalidity. In other words, two alternatives were put in place: 1) the thesis of the general prospect of considerable qualities for fraudulent error made it possible to include an ever-expanding list of cases likely to be invalidated, with extensive protection of the *deceptus*; 2) on the contrary, the thesis of the numerus clausus set itself as a formula aimed at avoiding extensive interpretations, potentially capable of extending excessively the number of qualities respect the fraudulent error (Bardi 1996). Other part of the doctrine was opposed to the introduction of the figure of the fraud in the category of impediments, propagating the thesis of the collocation of the code of *dolosa deceptio* between the matrimonial nullities (Punzi Nicolò 1971). Canonist Flatten argued that there was no need for the promulgation of a specific canon for the fraud, suggesting extending the discipline contained in canon 1083, in particular flanking the discipline of the fraudulent error to that of the *error personae et qualitatis*. This argument was based on the assumption that there was a causal link between the good and the quality concerned by the error, so that the *error qualitatis* would become of objective type (having regard to the personal quality of the other spouse whom it was subjected to stability of the *communitas coniugalis*), incident on the stability of the marital relationship and can create a false representation of the reality capable of determining the *deceptus* to the marriage celebration.

> Error circa qualitatem personae, etsi det cauam contractui matrimonium irritat tantum: 1. Si error qualitatis redundet in errorem personae; 2. Si persona libera matrimonium contrahat cum persona quam liberam putat, cum contra sit serva, servitute proprie dicta; 3. Si quis graviter ac fraudse alterius partis qualitate magni

momenti deceptus matrimonium ineat, quod re vere cognita non contraheret. (Flatten 1961, p. 18)

De Reina argued, however, that not all of the attentive conduct was relevant, but only the one capable of fraudulently misleading the intending spouse, with the purpose grant his matrimonial consensus. The author attempted to delimit the type of fraudulently caused errors, relevant for the purpose of a declaration of invalidity (De Reina 1967). According to a different point of view, Serrano relate the figure of the fraud to that of *vis et metus*, considering that the two cases of lack of consensus were generated by an external cause that forced the *deceptus* to provide a coerced consensus. According to this approach, guilty and error should be kept separate, being the fraud is a factor acting *ab extrinseco*. The difference between *metus* and fraud would consist of a clear perception, in the first case, of a distorted formation of will and consensus because of violent or frightening conduct, perception that is lacking in the case of the fraud where the *deceptus* is unaware of the suffered fraud and its disabling importance on consensus (Serrano Ruiz 1973).

Punzi assumed, on the contrary, a critical position with regard to the recognition of legal autonomy for the fraud, since the types of fraud are not homogeneous or referable to a common ratio, so that it would be unlawful to create a new head of nullity matrimonial. He, rather, proposed seeing again the whole systematics of the nullity matrimonial (Punzi Nicolò 1971).

Marcone, however, firmly argued that the only way to declare the nullity of a marriage drawn from the fraud was that of error, as between fraud and error there is a cause-effect relationship and a relationship of temporal succession in the sense that, to recognize a disabling effect on the fraud, it must first be said that the course of conduct has caused an erroneous representation of reality. Thus, according to A., It was not necessary to establish a self-standing juridical figure, but it was enough to extend the existing codification discipline (Marcone 1972).

On the other hand, for Giacchi (1973), fraud would be nothing more than a particular typology of error. Interesting is then the position of Villeggiante, which places a *distinguo* between pardon and error, believing that those who act under the influence of the fraud are *sub imperius alterius*. A. anticipates the need to include in the new discipline the case of *dolus causam dans* and *dolus qui inest contractui*, also arguing that fraudulent swindle induces an alteration of reality and, therefore, an error affecting the intellect of the contractor by effect of the error that strikes, on the contrary, the negotiating will. There is therefore a bond of subordination between error and fraud, since, if it were to fail the fraudulent conduct, the error would disappear and there would be no defect of will. For this reason, the two legal forms need a separate discipline, since, while leading *prima facie* to the same result, they have different characteristics (Villeggiante 1972). The doctrinal debate was somewhat lively during Vatican's Council II, but did not come to a conclusion about the configuration of the fraud in the context of the marriage relationship. This issue re-emerged in the revision of the Pio-Benedictine Code of 1917. Already during the first meetings of the *coetus consultorum*, the propensity to enter the figure of the fraud between the heads of nullity matrimonial, on the consideration of the existence of a cause-effect relationship between deceit and alteration of reality. Therefore, the gravity of the fraud is taken into account, which involves the need to examine the extent of the *deceptio dolosa*, not only to reference to the *animus decipiendi*, but also the objective intensity of the deceptive means. The Consultors were of the opinion that future discipline should provide for a qualified fraud in his ability to deceive and mislead a circumspect subject, for purpose of declaring nullity of matrimonial consent (Bardi 1996). In this way, by reporting misleading eligibility to the quality on which deception is concerned, the subjective criterion was linked to the objective, safeguarding the value of the institution of marriage. In 1977, the canon 300 of the *Schema De Matrimonio* was formulated: "*Qui matrimonium init deceptus fraud, ad obtinendum consensum patrato, circa aliquam alterius partis qualitatem, quae nata est ad consortium vitae coniugalis graviter perturbandum, invalide contahit*". The provision (the content of which will be reproduced largely by canon 1098 CIC 1983) focuses on the *deceptio dolosa* and onto intentionality of conduct of *decipiens* (which can also be identified with a third person) as well as on the disabling effect falling on the *consortium coniugale* and on the consent given, as there is an absolute incompatibility between deceptive conduct and the establishment of conjugal coexistence. The Consultors also posed the question of the relevance of omission conduct for the configurability of the fraud. Thus, the new and objective discipline, contained in the aforementioned canon 300, paves the way for the definition of the *ratio legis* of the institute of the fraud, consisting in the elimination of deception as an element preventing the formation of sincere and complete self-giving and in the need to safeguard the genuineness of the consent of the intending spouse. The conquest of the current 1098 its rest on the ratio in the attention to the person and the need for justice underlying the safeguard of the integrity of the consensus. Indeed, the legal institute of the dole paves the way for two different interpretations, depending on whether it is intended as a sanction of conduct of *deceptor*, or as a guarantee of marriage and matrimonial consent. A first orientation finds in the fraud a punitive intent of the deceptive conduct and the person of the *deceptor*. The

Legislator's reaction to unlawful conduct would be precisely the invalidity of the legal act influenced by the fraud (Fedele 1976). This thesis rests on an analogy with the discipline of *metus* and *vis*, since the act carried out under the influence of fear or violence is incapable of producing effects, being a breach of the freedom of choice of the intending spouse. The *ratio* of *vis* and *metus* would then be reflected in the repression of the *iniuira* and the *cogens* (the punitive purpose of the offense), as well as in the removal of a spoiled effect. At the same time, the discipline of the fraud would have a sanctions character of the deceptive conduct put in place by *decipiens* (Bardi 1996).

This type of approach has been strongly criticized in the light of the fact that the repression of the offense of *deceptor*, identified as the *ratio* of the discipline of the fraud, is unable to explain the section of the relevance of the deception in to serious cases in which it tends to snatch the matrimonial consensus or concerns the quality of the partner, which causes the conjugal life to be compromised. (Pompedda 1993). The paradox of the thesis, object of criticism, is found in the finding that the repression of the fraudulent conduct, in order to safeguard the matrimonial consensus, would lead to the conclusion that every type of deception deserves to be sanctioned, where the positive discipline referred to in the canon 1098 poses the objective conditions which void the fraud, thereby circumscribing the pathological evidence is to some deceptive conducts and not, indiscriminately, to any deceptive conduct. In other words, deception in itself must always be related to the effect on the victim, in terms of the falsification of reality or ignorance of the negative qualities of the spouse, not being able to compromise a priori the matrimonial consent (Gherro 1988). According to part of the jurisprudence (Decretum c. Serrano, 28. 05. 1982, in Monitor Ecclesiasticus, 108, 1983, 20–21) the *ratio* of the fraud should be perceived precisely in the distorting effect of the consent of the *decipiens*, which is immediately upstream of deception. In other words, the fraud would appear as an impedimental *conditio* for the communion of conjugal life, in that:

> the falsification of self-satisfaction – the subject of the matrimonial consensus – which is carried out with fraud: more than in the *deceptus* situation, whose matrimonial freedom is violated by the error in him caused by the deception of others, this ratio is seen in the lack of consensus of the *deceptus* – or anyway of the partner if the author of the fraud was a third – that instead of donating himself donates "aliquam speciem suispius, quae revera a realitate suae personae substantialiter differt". (Translation is mine: Moneta 1995, p. 157)

It seems, however, more respectful of the discipline given by canon 1098 to consider the *ratio* of the fraud in the need to safeguard the consensual freedom of the deceived contractor, since the norm is intended to ensure the proper formation of the voluntary process, which must be supported, at the base, by a perception of the object of consent as good and desirable and therefore not to be distorted. Fraudulent action, in fact, creates a false representation of reality in the intellect and affects the process of formation of the consent of the spouse. In other words, deceptive leads to *deceptus* a mistake in the intellect about the presence or absence of a given quality in the partner, resulting in an alteration of freedom, or at least a compromise on the freedom of choice. The central element in the fraud case is the voluntary intention of deceiving that concretises itself in the awareness of *alterum laedere* i.e. the intention to deceive a subject with the purpose of causing it to complete a legal act (matrimonial).

The basis of fraud must therefore be a fraudulent intent to obtain the consent of the *deceptus* (*ad obtinendum consensum patrate*), while other purposes appear irrelevant.

Suppose *animus decipiendi*, it is necessary that the purpose of deceptive conduct is to mislead the victim, in order to make them put into effect an act (the matrimonial consent) which otherwise would not have done. Canon 1098 CIC 1983 makes it relevant any form of fraud, both positive (falsifying reality) and negative (omission or silence on facts, qualities or circumstances that can represent the truth to the *deceptus*). The end is therefore to snatch the consent of the deceived spouse, prejudging the will with an error of assessment. The discipline of the code does not qualify the figure of the *deceptus*, which can well be identified as third person in relation to the intending spouses, which could organize the deception in autonomy or in agreement with one of the future spouses, which could organize the deception in autonomy or in agreement with one of the future spouses, despite the victim, whose legal status deserves protection and protection, has suffered the effects of wicked deception and tensed to conspire matrimonial (Punzi Nicolò 1981).

The correct interpretation of the positive norm mentioned in the aforementioned canon 1098 militates in the sense of rendering invalid the fraudulent conduct of a third person, which gives rise to a cause of vice of conjugal consent. The deception of the third party is not in itself an anti-Juridical one, but it maintains its suitability, even *ab externo*, to generate error or ignorance in the hands of the deceived spouse.

Gravity around which Deceptive Behavior Rotates

On the point two different orientations appear: a first one thinks that the deceitful conduct should be valued in objective, such sense to report the gravity of the fraud to his fitness of changing the perception of the reality in the intending spouses or in the intending spouse; in this sense the fraud assumes significance only if fit to induce in error the intending spouse or to make persisting in him a state of ignorance about the existence or the absence of a determinate quality (desired or not appreciated), afferent the person of the other consort (Palombi 2001).

The second approach is to assess the severity of the fraud in relation to the person circumvented, depending on whether he is an avowed and prudent person or an inattentive person "Such a deceptive ability, however, does not have to be commensurate with the objective criterion, as traditionally identified in *vir prudens*, but precisely because this provision is primarily concerned with the protection of the freedom of the contractors according to a subjective criterion commensurate with the person of the *deceptus*. Fraudulent conduct must be implemented by means capable of making an individual mistakenly fall as one who is intended to deceive in the concrete case" (translation is mine. Bonnet 1985, pp. 85–86).

Both of these arguments appear to be criticized: the first, since the assessment of the degree of intensity of fraud on the sole objective criterion risks to hold as irrelevant all the deceptive conduct that leads to the error of a distracted or inexperienced subject; The second interpretation, however, entails the risk of believing that no serious fraudulent conduct triggers deception, since the only subjective criterion, based on the mental ease of the deceived victim, leads to the consequence of not giving legal weight to behaviors connoted by a certain *gravitas:*

"It would be *gravis* the fraud that *cadet in virum prudentem.* Even in this case, one must wonder whether the canon lawmaker can safely accept the proposal that would end up damaging the less aware, simple man, the naive man, but he was entitled to marriage *iure naturae* and its protection. [...] There would be discrimination, whose injustice would find the foundation in natural right". (Translation is mine: Fagiolo 1972, p. 85)

In fact, it would be useful to find an intermediate solution between the two opposing theories examined, so that both the *deceptus* and the *deceptor* position can be evaluated. The deceit put in place by the *deceptor*, in order to take disability, must have prevented the knowledge of the *deceptus* truth. It is also necessary to evaluate the fraudulent behavior, the means used to

designate deception and eligibility *ad alterum decipiendi*. As far as fraudulent behavior is concerned, there is a distinction between fraudulent and
omission of fraud: the first consists of an active behavior of *deceptor*
composed of *"facendo aliquid vel dicendo quo aliter in errorem dicitur"*
(Michelis 1965, p. 660); the second, is represented by a negative conduct
consisting of reticence or silence on negative qualities. Commitment
fraud causes a fraudulent error as it creates a falsification of reality, omission fraud acts on a status of previous ignorance about the existence or
absence of certain qualities, increasing it. In order to analyse the impact
of omission fraud on the validity of consent given by a spouse, it should
be noted that the *post-novum codicem* doctrine (Pompedda, 1995) it seems
compatible to believe that negative behavior is also invalidate, where it
may be considered fraudulent or otherwise supported by *intentio decipiendi*
and is intended to expose the consent of the spouse. The *ratio* of the
theory examined has to be found in the right of each subject to be able to
express a free and conscious double wish, which corresponds with the
other spouse's duty to acquaint the partner with the presence or absence
of a desired, unsuccessful quality , which could seriously put the *consortium vitae coniugalis* into crisis. Another issue to be considered is the legal
causal link between the swindles of *deceptor* and the consents of the
deceptus. And indeed, fraud can be categorized or as *dolus causam dans* (or
decisive or direct fraud), in the absence of which the *deceptus* would never
have been determined to perform the legal act, or as *dolus incidens*, which
occurs when Perceived deception is not of such intensity as to interfere
with the consent of the *deceptus*, who would have opted, even in the
absence of the fraud, to marry. The Legislator, both in canon 125, §2, and
in canon 1098, does not consider the distinction examined of two types
of frauds, since the *dolus incidens* produce, in the matrimonial field, give
legal relevance to any justification, also affecting the will, is not perceived
by the subject as the determinant of his consensus. This would cause
excessive dilation of the field of fraud-related disabilities, becoming relevant to any type of swindle, also concerning irrelevant qualities of the
spouse, with the consequence that a declaration of nullity of marriage
would a be possible, if the intending spouse equally desired it, if at the
time of the celebration, had known the truth not affected by the fraud.
For this reason, the Legislator has decided to give relevance only to the
dolus causam dans, aimed at *obtinendum consensum patrate*. It is therefore
necessary legally framed the subject of fraudulent conduct addressed to
snatch the spouse's marriage consent. It consists, in accordance with the
Code's instructions, in the quality of the other side, which by its nature
may seriously disturb the married life community. The same can be physical and moral and must be connected to the partner. It is also necessary
for the *deceptus* to be convinced of his true presence. This quality can

objectively determine the subject and can, by the will of intending spouse, assume the qualification of 'uniqueness', while in reality it remains ordinary. This influence may occur at *ante* or *post*-date to marriage (and in this case, the latter will not be declared null), and only *ante* and therefore it will be necessary to assess case by case the disruption, that the quality may have generated in the consortium. I would therefore consider that quality cannot only be an objective feature, since it may materially deteriorate the behavior of all life but also subjective, since it may have been 'experienced' in various ways by the deceived intending spouse. In other words, it is necessary to evaluate how the swindle may influence the *decisum* of the *deceptus*, taking into account its own mental form and personal lifestyle.

Conclusions

As you can see, the fraud can present a subjective and objective legal identity, which determines matrimonial nullity. I would now consider it necessary to analyse the question of retroactivity of the legal case of fraud, in order to determine whether the discipline currently provided for in Canon 1098 applies to marriages before its entry into effectiveness.

It must first be stated that in canonical law there are two types of rules: 1) Divine origin, which have a perennial application as they result from revelation; 2) those promulgated by ecclesiastical law and that produce their effects only from the moment of their promulgation. To answer the question, part of the doctrine and jurisprudence (Navarrete 1987, Parisella, 24 March 1983, in *Monitor Ecclesiasticus*, 108, 1983, 491, 4) considers that fraud is human right and therefore , so not retroactive. The same thesis states that in order to demonstrate its divine origin, it is necessary to refer cases in which there is a lack of absolute will and not about cases where there is a mere vice of consensus. To this is added that the reason why, given its divine aspect, the fraud was contemplated so late, that is, just in the CIC '83. Ultimately, if the fraud provoked a complete lack of consensus and not a vice, it would not be understandable the wording of §2 of can.125 which, as stated above, recognizes the validity of the fraudulent act, with certain exceptions being made not by divine law, but by ecclesiastical law. In this regard, the Pontifical Commission for the Interpretation of Legislative Texts argues:

> The Constitutional Court is inclined to consider the will of the can. 1098 of merely positive law and therefore not retroactive. However, given the wide variety of cases that might fall under the circumstances described therein, it cannot be ruled out that some of them may constitute nullity arising from natural law, in the event

that an affirmative judgment would be legitimate. It corresponds to the judges, in possession of all the possible elements, to assess whether in the concrete case there is a kind of invalidating error consent not for the positive disposition of the can. 1098 but by virtue of natural law, as has been the case in some judgments before the promulgation of the Code. (Translation is mine: The passage was taken from the judgment in Ragni, 19. 12. 1995, in ARRT, 87, 1998, 720, n.8)

Otherwise oriented are the doctrinal and jurisprudential practice (De Filippi, 4 December 1997, in ARRT, 89, 2002, 856, 5, c Serrano, 25. 10. 1996, in ARRT, 88, 1999, 650–651, n.4), which support the retroactivity of fraud as the deception would adversely affect the *consortium vitae coniugalis*; this would lead to the radical incompatibility between *deceptio* and valid consensus (Bardi 1996). For these reasons,

the disposition of can. 1098 does not constitute a positive determination of the human legislator, but an act of directing to genuinely declare a principle of natural divine law, albeit formally new, it cannot therefore apply to every marriage, at any time celebrated, subjected to judgment of the Courts of the Church. (Translation is mine: Giacchi 1973, p. 245)

In the same direction moves Pompedda, who believes that natural law "at least on the cognitive level, undergoes an evolutionary development and improvement through the rational contribution of culture and also through the deepening of the theological or dogmatic data [...] the fact that only later, and not from the beginning, the legislature has devoted a provision to this particular vice does not exclude [...] its relevance to divine law, and hence its applicability without any limitation of temporal efficacy" (translation is mine. Pompedda 1987, p. 538). I would agree with the second approach, as the subject of 1098 is not the mere consensual vice but the non-existence of the conjugal consortium, as the spouse is found, to be married to the partner who, in reality, is different from what he really wanted. Consequently, to have affected not only is consent, but the very existence of sacramental marriage. The fact that the exceptions of can. 125, §2 are laid down by ecclesiastical law does not elude the question of the divine origin of fraud, since the sacrament of marriage, as seen elsewhere, provides for the full consciousness of intending spouses (which must not be deceived). Indeed, I may think that this §2, given the divine derivation of fraud, believes that the fraudulent act cannot be affected if the consensus is not fully conditioned by its swindle. Relevant exceptions to can. Divine law then leaves canon 125 to the discretion of ecclesiastical law. To try the fraud, first you need to focus on the action and the fraudulent intention, as well as on the quality that you intend to undermine and the mistake on which the intending spouse is fallen. Not to forget is the reaction that the latter has when it discovers the truth and can affect the salvation and continuation of the marriage agreement (D'Auria 2007).

References

Bardi M. (1966) *Il dolo nel matrimonio canonico*. Giuffré, Milano.

De Reina V. (1967) *Error y dolo en el matrimonio*. Pamplona.

Bonnet P.A. (1985) *Introduzione al consenso matrimoniale canonico*. Giuffré, Milano.

D'Auria A. (2007) *Il consenso matrimoniale. Dottrina e giurisprudenza canonica*, Aracne, Roma, pp.323–369.

Garcia Martin J. (1999). *Le norme generali del Codex Iuris Canonici*, Marcianum, Roma.

Fagiolo V. (1972) "La trattazione del problema del fraud in seno al Concilio Vaticano II". In AA.VV. *Il dolo del consenso matrimoniale*, II, Città del Vaticano, p. 85.

Fedele P. (1941) *Discorso generale sull'ordinamento canonico*. Cedam, Padova.

Fedele P. (1964) "Dolo (dir. can.)". In *Enciclopedia del Diritto*, vol. XII. Giuffré, Milano, pp. 804–805.

Ferrata G. B. (1972) "Il dolo nella celebre sentenza Versalien". In AA.VV. *Il dolo nel consenso matrimoniale*, Città del Vaticano, pp. 141–142.

Flatten H. (1961) *Quomodo matrimonium contrahentes iure canonico contra doli tutandi sint*, Colonia, 18.

Garcia Martin J. (1999) *Le norme generali del Codex Iuris Canonici*. Marcianum, Roma.

Gherro S. (1988) *Diritto matrimoniale canonico*. Cedam, Padova.

Giacchi O. (1973) *Il consenso nel matrimonio canonico*, Giuffré, Milano.

Mantovani M. (1972) "Sull'impedimentum doli". In AA.VV. *Il dolo nel consenso matrimoniale*, Città del Vaticano, pp. 111–112.

Marcone G. (1972) "Considerazioni sul dolo e sull'errore nel consenso matrimoniale e schema di canone". In AA.VV. *Il dolo nel consenso matrimoniale*, Città del Vaticano, p. 107.

Moneta P. (1995) *Il matrimonio nel nuovo diritto canonico*. Ecig, Genova.

Navarrete U. (1987) "Canon 1098 de errore doloso estne iuris naturali an iuris positivi Ecclesiae". In *Periodica*, 76, p. 179.

Palombi R. (2001) *Errore doloso e atto giuridico*. In AA.VV. *Errore e dolo nella giurisprudenza della Rota Romana*, Città del Vaticano, p. 68.

Pompedda M.F. (1993) "Annotazioni sul diritto matrimoniale nel nuovo codice canonico". In POMPEDDA M.F. *Studi di diritto matrimoniale canonico*. Milano, Giuffré, p. 226.

Pompedda M.F. (1995) "*Le problematiche di diritto canonico in relazione all'AIDS*". In *Il Diritto Ecclesiastico*, 1995, I, 779.

Pompedda M.F. (1987) *"Il can. 1095 del nuovo C.I.C. fra elaborazione precodiciale e prospettive di sviluppo interpretativo"*. In *Ius Canonicum*, 37, p. 538.

Punzi Nicolò A. M. (1971) *"Il dolo nel matrimonio canonico in una prospettiva di riforma del Codex"*. In *Il Diritto Ecclesiastico*, 82, I, p. 590.

Punzi Nicolò A. M. (1981) "Problematica attuale dell'errore e del dolo nel matrimonio". In *Ephemerides Juris Canonici*, 37, p. 160.

Serrano Ruiz J.M. (1973) "El dolo en el consentimiento matrimonial". In *Revista Espanola de Derecho Canònico*, 29, pp. 184–185.

Villeggiante S. (1972) "Per l'impostazione della rilevanza del dolo", In AA.VV. *Il dolo nel consenso matrimoniale*, Città del Vaticano, 49.

8

The Importance of the *error iuris* in Issuing the Matrimonial Consensus

CIRO PUNZO

Consistency of the Error of Law

Canon 1099 CIC 1983 states textually: "*Error circa matrimonii unitatem vel indissolubilitatem aut sacramentalem dignitatem, dummodo non determinet voluntatem, non vitiat consensum matrimonialem*". The discipline just described is extremely complex and is the result of various interpretations that recognize legal autonomy in the present case. The legal aspect of *iuris error* is often accompanied by other disabling forms of matrimonial consent (ignorance, exclusion). Therefore, an analysis of the norm referred to in canon 1099 cannot disregard a comparison with the rules laid down in canons 1096 and 1101. From such a comparison, it will be possible to rule on the existence or not of an operational autonomy of the error of law under the current law on matrimonial nullity. In this regard, canon 1096 recites: "*1. In order to have a matrimonial consensus, it is necessary for the contractors to at least not ignore that marriage is the permanent community between man and woman, ordained to procreate the offspring through some sexual co-operation. 2. This ignorance is not presumed after puberty*" (translation is mine). As for his 'colleague', can. 1101, rule: "*1. the inner consensus of the mind is assumed to conform to the words or signs used to celebrate the marriage 2. But if one or both parties exclude with a positive act of will the wedding itself, or any essential element or an essential property, the contract in an invalid way*" (translation is mine).

In primis, a distinction must be made between ignorance and the error of law, as Pellegrino argues:

"It has been found that ignorance and error, as far as they have some affinity, and sometimes even a certain connection and inter-dependence, are distinct concepts with their own content and meaning; and it has been added that ignorance is the lack of proper knowledge (*carentia scientiae debitae*), error is an inexact, flawed knowledge; a false judgment (*falsum iudicium*) but that there is always a part of ignorance in error and ignorance, in turn, is the cause of error and explicates its effectiveness as it becomes a mistake; with the consequence that theoretically the error can be considered a subtype of ignorance". (Translation is mine: Pellegrino 1997, pp. 364–365)

The correlation between canon 1096 and canon 1099 is according to Bonnet: "a serious hermeneutic problem due to the duplicity of the norms enshrined in the code concerning the error of law. In addition to the legally relevant error and concerning, the essence sanctioned in can. 1096 §1 CIC '83, there is another, established in can.1099 CIC, related to the essential properties and the sacramentality, which, as long as it does not enter the intellectual moment that determines the will of the marriage, does not induce the invalidity of the *matrimonium in fieri*. This issue is further complicated not only by what the canon 1099 can do about the relevance of error on essential properties and sacramental-ity when informing the will, but also by the disposition of the canon 1101, §2 CIC '83, which provides for matrimonial nullity when there is an exclusion made with a positive act of will for both conditions – essence and essential properties – that for the mistake were distinct, in fact, in the one and the nell 'Another case, with even opposite conse-quences with regard to the invalidity of the act" (translation is mine. Bonnet 1995, pp. 34–35). The distinction between the essence (and even identity) and the essential properties of the marital shop emerges with cogency: "Essence is what identifies a thing in itself, including all the elements necessary to constitute it and identify it in its entity, dis-tinguishing it from everything else. Essence is what conforms to one thing for what it is". Instead, the essential properties: "while not consti-tuting the essence of things and thus distinguishing themselves from the latter, they are necessarily connected with the essence itself, not by forming it into what it is, but by identifying it in relation to any other entity. Essence does not express property, nevertheless requires it insur-mountably. In other words, an essence would not be what it is, if it did not have certain properties. Moreover, properties, as qualifications, are in no way capable of subsisting alone but can only be incorporated into an essence, not concretizing it for what it is, but typing it in an indis-pensable way in its existentiality. Essence and essential properties are *distinguishable* elements between them" (translation is mine: Bonnet 1995, p. 28). It is necessary; however, to point out that, although distinct, properties (according to the best ontological doctrine) depend on essence, is characterized by the same. At this point, it should be noted that since Canon 1057 stipulates that the consent of the intending spouses must be explicitly expressed and aimed at the constitution of the *consortium totius vitae*, it could not deny the existence of a strong correlation between essence and essential properties. In fact, the desire to strongly, want something means directing your attention and will to an essence with its properties. It may happen that the intending spouse desires the essence, but not, for lack of information, one of its properties. It thus follows "a determination of the will resulting from an erroneous knowledge so that it models the will and presupposes a specific intentionality of the relationship at the constitutive moment of the marriage that will be realized" (translation is mine: Bonnet 1995, p. 53).

The two reasons for matrimonial nullity referred to in canons 1096 and 1099 are to be considered distinct and autonomous by object, which is wider in the provision in canon 1096, since we are faced with the identity of the marriage must be known from the intending spouse because the marriage will be valid, at the time of the constituent act the bond (Pellegrino 1997); instead, canon 1099 has a more limited object identificated with the essential properties of marriage, which concern matrimonial substance. It therefore appears evident that if the two cases have a different object, they will also be disciplined in a different way: "canon 1096, 1 CIC refers to the relationship between knowledge and essence, expressing the insurmountable need for such awareness" (translation is mine: Bonnet 1995, 36); instead, in the error of law, the will of the intending spouse who is mistakenly informed about the essential properties, but not about the essence of marriage is emphasized. A doctrinal and jurisprudential orientation dating back to the Benedictine Plan codification of 1917 proposes an approach between the case of the error of law and the cases of exclusion referred to in canon 1101, §2, in the event that the error is of a such intensity as to prevent a conation other than that caused by the false will. Then the *error*:

> given its profound and pertinent rooting, passes from the intellect in the context of the will, determining the real and true content of the consent of the contractor, who, by radical influence of this particular mistake, wants a marriage positively and voluntarily devoid of unity, indissolubility, or sacramentality. In this case, the error is no longer easy, in fact passing through to being a decisive mistake in the content of the inner act of the will, causes in it an objective and positive absence of unity, indissolubility or sacra-

mentality of true and valid marriage. (Translation is mine: Benigni 1999, pp. 154–155)

Such a legal argument, however, implies that the invalidity of the matrimonial consensus results not from the error of law, but from the positive will of the contractor, who finds in the error itself a reason for excluding the essential properties of marriage (*causa simulandi remota*). In other words, the intending spouse not want the essential properties, even knowing the marriage properties. Instead, the different discipline contained in canon 1099 presupposes that the intending spouse did not know the marital property and set in its mind a marriage pattern other than that proposed by the Church. Part of the doctrine in this regard considers that between the figure of the decisive error the will, or, ultimately, determining a defect of will, and the figure of the positive act of will capable of concretizing the simulation phenomenon, not only there is diversity but even incompatibility: error and simulation are two logical and practically different juridical categories, and such that they do not allow the conversion of one or their simultaneous coexistence, in the sense that where there is an error excluding the will of a matrimonial, there is no place for the simulation (i.e. for the exclusionary will) (Villeggiante 1984). It should also be stated that the error of law would not require an express manifestation of the intending spouse, since it ignores the element that is going to exclude. In this regard, part of the doctrine states the non – application of

a positive act, in the sense of traditional doctrine, since the element that is excluded will not be known [...] This statement [...] seems to me to be very relevant [...] above all because it responds to incomparable logic: on the one hand, in the cases of decisive error, we have a deficient intellectual representation; on the other hand, we have a will that, while not ignoring, but being mistaken does not want to exclude it, as much as a wrong object ... as long as the relevance of the error in the mind of the intending spouse is such that it is invincible, an erroneous, that is, no positive act is placed on the subject of marriage. If, however, the party has an awareness of opposition between what it believes to be true and the truth proclaimed by the Church, then error is transformed into simulation and erroneous beliefs become the next and the remote cause of the simulation. In this case, can be presented to the will the possibility of choice, and therefore it can be 'positively' accepted or excluded, explicitly or implicitly. (Translation is mine: Benigni 1999, pp. 157–158)

To Influence or Affect the Marriage Decision what Degree of Intensity of *error iuris* is Required?

The problem is the following: it has been noticed in can. 1097, §2 CIC '83, how important is the influence of the personal quality of intending spouse. In this case not only must we return to personal quality, but focus attention on the conditioning of intending spouse through cultural and social influences.

The doctrine, in this regard, highlights three possible types of error:

(1) The intending spouse is mistakenly convinced that marriage is not monogamous and indissoluble, but even if the latter had these characteristics, he would have married equally. In this case, the marriage will be valid. Part of the doctrine believes that "the first degree constitutes the error – in a sense 'peaceful' – that exists only in the sphere of the intellect and does not affect the concrete strong-willed choices" (translation is mine: Grocholewsky 1995, p. 14). In that regard, I would think that we are in the presence of a simple mistake, which does not affect the consensus. In other words, the mistake remains in the intellect and does not cause any consequences in the will of the intending spouse and so he correct the mentioned error, manifesting his intention to embrace the sacramental conjugal pact;

(2) The second degree of error consists not only in the conviction that marriage does not have certain properties, but also in the attitude (not conjugal), that it puts into being. In other words, for example, the intending spouse is convinced that marriage is not unique and therefore he wants more agreements conjugal contemporary or successive. This error, unlike the first one, does not only stop in the intellect but continues in the attitude and in the related decision. In this case, we are faced with a remote simulation, but we still do not have the application in the canon that we are dealing with.

Part of the doctrine believes that the second degree

is when error does not only exist in the sphere of the intellect but in some degree also deforms the habitual attitude of the will. This error is defined in several ways: habitual intention, habitual will, inclination of will, disposition of will, generic intention, generic will, persistent error, consolidated error, tenacious error [...] These are people who not only have misguided ideas about the essential properties of marriage, but they also actually do something against such property [...] Although it is an attitude of will, expressed in concrete acts, it is not enough to render marriage void because [...] it only applies to marriage in general, not its actual matrimonial consensus, determining its object. (Translation is mine: Grocholewsky 1995, p. 14)

In this case, the will of the intending spouse does not determine his consent, as it does not yet realize any conjugal pact.

(3) The third degree of error falls within the scope of our canon, since the intending spouse contracts the conjugal pact with the full conviction that, for example, the same is not indissoluble. In other words, if he had known this characteristic, he would not have contracted a marriage bond. We are in presence of a strong mistake, "which already contains the positive exclusion of an essential element. It would be people so profoundly distorted by the mistake about an essential property of marriage they acquire by contracting marriage – any marriage – positively they cannot want no other constraint than that corresponding to their mistake" (translation is mine: Grocholewsky 1980, pp. 594–596). In the latter case "the judgment of practical reason don't proposes more of one type of conjugal bond for the marriage to be founded, because it does not deliberate and does not know any other [...] in this case the will becomes self-determined doing own the only matrimonial content that its practical reason makes it known and proposes them as a conjugal union to realize in his life. The subject [...] if he decides to marry, in this case, the only assessment that practical reason proposes to him on conjugal bond is necessarily the only type of concrete bond he can choose and want his will [...] If this only practical judgment of reason turns out to be a mistake on property or sacramentality, then such a mistake has determined the will to want, as a good thing to be realized with conjugal bond, a kind of false and perverse conjugation, that is, without truth and objective goodness according to the Church". (Translation is mine: Viladrich 2001, pp. 243–244)

In this case, then, we are in the presence of a spoiled consent *ab origine*, because the will only considers the wrong conviction of the intellect.

Ultimately, I would think that the error of law might have a subjective and objective connotation. The first is characterized by 'false conviction of marriage', erroneously attributing it to absolute certainty. Consequently, the same becomes the cause – the defect of the act of will.

Having this conviction, the objective connotation of the marriage contract, that is, its characteristics, is affected. In other words, the intending spouse is convinced that marriage is not unique, indissoluble, or sacramental. In fact, the mistake

> "becomes [...] recognizable, as the proof of his passage to the act of will must point out that it is a wrong-headed error, motivating the choice of marriage, and resulting in the act of will, that is, the concrete choice of false object proposed by it contrary to that defined by the canonical marriage order, through such an occasion that causes the passage of error into a strong-willed sphere". (Translation is mine: Stankiewicz 2003, p. 232)

Conclusion

I could conclude by claiming that the error of law is a matter of autonomous nullity, which could not be part of the simulation, as it states part of the doctrine that it believes that "...canon 1099 is therefore to come to the more general figure of the voluntary exclusion of the substantive content of marriage, of what the traditional doctrine indicated as '*intentio contra matrimonii substantiam*' and that in judicial practice is also commonly referred to as a simulation" (translation is mine: Moneta 1995, pp. 114–115), since while in the latter, the intending spouse, knowing the real characteristics of the matrimonial institute, acquired or because it has received a Catholic education or sacraments, or belongs to a Christian family, manifests a simulation act when it states, for example, ignorance of the property of the conjugal pact, in the error of law the intending spouse, for an objective knowledge, falls into the above-mentioned error. The interpretation of the writer also deviates from the condition (in which another part of the doctrine would want to make the error of the law: "In fact, the condition is a specification of the object of consent by means of a preferential act of will towards an object rather than another. In our case, in the implicit exclusion there is a preference for marriage, configured according to the wrong mentality of true marriage. This prevalence of will is implied in the fact that the two objects – the true marriage and the pseudo-marriage – are mutually exclusive and, consequently, in directing a positive act of will towards one of them, it is preferred to the other" (translation is mine: Serres López De Guereñu 1998, pp. 347–348; Navarrete 1992, p. 490), since in the same there is the same full knowledge and awareness of the properties of the matrimonial institute, which is not present in the epigraph argument. Precisely this non-knowledge cannot require an express manifestation of will concerning the exclusion of matrimonial properties and, consequently, canon 1099 is 'sacrificed', I would think unjustly, in the probative aspect of the simulation. Then through worthy witnesses of faith, we try to prove the lack of knowledge of the intending spouse about the mentioned properties. I would argue otherwise that canon 1099 could be demonstrated 'autonomously', trying to investigate, also using the witnesses mentioned, that Christian experience of the intending spouse, which qualifies himself as 'ignorant' (D'Auria 2007).

References

Benigni S. (1999) *La simulazione implicita: aspetti sostanziali e processuali*. Pontificia Università Lateranense, Tesi, Roma.

Bonnet P.A. (1995) "L'errore di diritto sulle proprietà essenziali e sulla sacramentalità". In AA.VV. *Error determinans voluntatem (Can. 1099)*, Città del Vaticano, p. 28.

D'Auria A. (2007) *Il consenso matrimoniale. Dottrina e giurisprudenza canonica*, Aracne, Roma, pp. 369–407.

Grocholewski Z. (1995) "L'errore circa l'unità, l'indissolubilità e la sacramentalità del matrimoni". In AA.VV., *Error determinans voluntatem (Can. 1099)*, Città del Vaticano, p. 14.

Grocholewski Z. (1980) "Relatio inter errorem et positivam indissolubilitatis exclusionem in nuptiis contrahendis". In *Periodica*, 69, pp. 594–596.

Moneta P. (1995) *Il matrimonio nel nuovo diritto canonico*. Ecig, Genova.

Navarrete U. (1992) *"De sensu clausolae 'dummodo non determinet voluntatem' can. 1099"*. In *Periodica*, 81, p. 490.

Pellegrino P. (1997) *L'errore di diritto nel matrimonio canonico*. In *Il Diritto Ecclesiastico*, 109, pp. 364–365.

Serres López De Guereñu R. (1998) "Error recidens in condizionem sine qua non (Can 126). Studio storico – giuridico". In *Periodica*, 87, pp. 347–348.

Stankiewicz A. (2003) "L'autonomia giuridica dell'errore di diritto determinante la volontà". In AA.VV., *"Diritto matrimoniale canonico"*, vol. II, *Il consenso*, Città del Vaticano, p. 232.

Viladrich P.J. (2001) *Il consenso matrimoniale. Tecniche di qualificazione e di esegesi della cause canoniche di nullità (cc. 1095–107 CIC)*, Giuffrè, Milano, pp. 243–244.

Villeggiante S. (1984) *"Errore e volontà simulatoria nel consenso matrimoniale in diritto canonico"*. In *Monitor Ecclesiasticus*, 109, pp. 494–495.

The Editor and Contributors

Silvia Dell'Orco Ph.D.
is an italian psychologist. Her research is conducted in the field of the psychology of reasoning and decision making, cognitive neuroscience and clinical psychology. She is author and co-author of many articles in scientific journals.

Nelson Mauro Maldonato
is an italian Psychiatrist, professor at University of Naples Federico II. He has been a visiting professor at Duke University, at Universidade de São Paulo (USP) and Pontifícia Universidade Católica (PUC) of São Paulo. He is an author and curator of volumes and scientific articles published in numerous languages. He is also the scientific director of International Research Week.

Luca Bartoli
is an italian Psychiatrist. He contributed to the preparation of the Italian version of the Criteria of the International Classification of Mental Diseases (ICD – 10th edition, Chapter V).

Raffaele Sperandeo Ph.D.
is an italian Psychiatrist, Psychotherapist, Professor and Director of SiPGI (School of Gestalt Psychotherapy Integrated). He is author and co-author of many articles in scientific journals.

Ciro Punzo
is a lawyer, a law graduate and Juris Doctor Canonici at the Pontifical Lateran University; he was admitted to a Ph.D. degree in Economics and Political Sciences at the Sophia University Institute. He is currently a Professor at ISSR 'S.Roberto Bellarmino' Capua (Ce). He is enrolled in the second year of the Rotary Studio course and is the author of monographs and many articles in scientific journals.

Daniela Iennaco
is a Psychologist and Research Fellow at SiPGI (School of Gestalt Psychotherapy Integrated); her degree was taken at the Department of Clinical Psychology.

Nicole Nascivera

is an italian Psychologist and Phenomenologist Psychotherapist, Professor at SiPGI (School of Gestalt Psychotherapy Integrated). She is co-author of many articles in scientific journals.

www.ingramcontent.com/pod-product-compliance
Lightning Source LLC
Chambersburg PA
CBHW050617280326
41932CB00016B/3082